PATTERNED *by* GRACE

How Liturgy Shapes Us

DANIEL T. BENEDICT JR.

UPPER ROOM BOOKS®
NASHVILLE

See page 158 for an extension of the copyright page.

Cover design: Tobias' Outerwear for Books
Cover image: © Royalty-free/Corbis
Interior design: Nancy Terzian/nterdesign.com
First printing: 2007

Library of Congress Cataloging-in-Publication

Benedict, Daniel T.
Patterned by grace : how liturgy shapes us / Daniel T. Benedict, Jr.
    p. cm.
Includes bibliographical references.
ISBN-13: 978-0-8358-9905-5
ISBN-10: 0-8358-9905-5
1. Liturgies. 2. Public worship. 3. Spiritual life—Christianity. I. Title.
BV198.B435 2006
264—dc22

2006030002

Printed in the United States of America

To Char, Marion, Elsie, Bob, and Charlotte,
who loved God in the liturgy

CONTENTS

ACKNOWLEDGMENTS

So many persons have been my mentors, colleagues, and friends in the journey that led to this book. Some are very much alive on terra firma, and some are, as the traditional Festival of Nine Lessons and Carols puts it, on "another shore and in a greater light." I name them in somewhat chronological order and with deep gratitude: Robert Mitchell, Char Stohlman, William Beasley, J. Ernest Rattenbury, Evelyn Underhill, James F. White, Marion Newcomb, David Young, Conrad Hoover, Hoyt Hickman, Don Saliers, L. Edward Phillips, Laurence Stookey, E. Byron Anderson, Robert B. Davis, Lee Cunningham, Fred Edie, Mary Alice McKinney, Alan Detscher, Karen Ward, Karen Westerfield Tucker, Dean McIntyre, Safiyah Fosua, Barbara Day Miller, Gordon Lathrop, members of the Order of Saint Luke, and the people of God in various churches who have been bold to live the liturgy deeply with me. Their passions, yearnings, and brilliance as people who pray the liturgy and reflect upon the church's experience of liturgical prayer are woven throughout this book, whether specifically named or not.

These chapters first took shape as lectures to Spiritual Formation Academy 20 at Sumatanga Conference Center in Alabama in October 2003. I am grateful to that group of seekers for their participation in the lectures and to Jerry Haas, director of The Upper Room Academy for Spiritual Formation, and JoAnn Miller of Upper Room Books, for their encouragement to turn the lectures into a book.

Jean Musterman, staff assistant to the worship directors in the Center for Worship Resourcing at the General Board of Discipleship, was a lifesaver in researching sources during a period when I was in limbo between Nashville and Hawaii.

My journey companion, Mary O, has been a consistent and intimate dialogue partner and a means of grace for keeping my feet near the ground when I tended toward liturgical ideology more than pastoral theology.

Of all of these I say with the church, "God is glorious in the saints. Thanks be to God."

Trinity Sunday 2006

INTRODUCTION

We were vacationing in the Jemez Mountains of northern New Mexico. Near our campsite that Fourth of July, day picnickers were playing a heated and energetic softball game. Mary O, my life companion and spouse, struck up a conversation with one of the spectators. In the course of the conversation, she mentioned some distinctively beautiful sculptures she had seen at the Indian Pueblo Cultural Center in Albuquerque a few days before. The woman said that her husband had some of his work in that center and asked if Mary O would like to meet him. When the game was over, the woman introduced them. As they talked, Mary O discovered that this man had created the sculpted pieces she had so admired. He appreciatively received Mary O's affirmation and asked if she would like to come to his studio to see more of his work. Delighted, she accepted the invitation.

A few days later, she and a friend went to his home and studio. There she viewed more of the beautiful, deeply centered work she had seen earlier and some large pieces of raw stone. She asked the sculptor how he knew what to create from the stone. He told her that he sat and looked at the stone, listening for it to tell him what it wanted to be. In other words, a communion took place between the rock and the sculptor. Rather than setting out to impose an arbitrary shape upon the stone, he collaborated with the stone. The stone shaped the sculptor's mind and spirit as much as the sculptor shaped the stone. The sculpting process became a collaborative engagement over time, gradually revealing what the stone would become. The sculptor heeded the "will" of the stone and allowed it to shape his vision and perspective. As I listened to the story, I mused that this collaborative process was an imaginative, risky, and life-releasing venture.

Likewise, Christian worship is a collaborative engagement over time, in which the living God and the people of God "listen" to each other and are shaped in love around each other. It too is an imaginative, risky, and life-shaping venture.

This book offers an invitation to listen more deeply to something we Christians do week in and week out, year in and year out, over a lifetime. By attending deeply, we can develop a greater appreciation for how worship shapes our lives. It may appear that worship is all about what *we* do: we gather; we sing; we pray; we read and hear the scriptures; we listen to sermons; we raise concerns for others; we offer ourselves and our resources to God; we embrace; we give thanks and eat sacred food; we scatter into the world. Sometimes we get wet together or remember when we got wet. Daily we hallow life and the morning with prayer and the evening with praise. We remember the story of God's deliverance from slavery, sin, and death in Israel and in Christ, following a calendar of seasons. Worship seems to be what we do, something we shape.

But there is another way to look at worship. Though on the

surface worship may appear to be our doing, at a deeper level and in the long view, it is the work of the triune God in and through us. In our doing God prompts us to listen more deeply to what the "rock," our shield and the horn of our salvation (Ps. 18:2), is calling us to be. In worship God shapes our lives and transforms us "from one degree of glory to another" as we behold God (2 Cor. 3:18), source of all, eternal Word and Holy Spirit. In worship our visions, desires, attitudes, yearnings, wills, and lives are recast, molded, and shaped to conform to the dying and rising of Christ for the life of the world. I invite you to enter more deeply into worship as the work of the Holy Spirit through Jesus Christ to the glory of God. This book beckons you to see yourself as part of a great work that is imaginative, risky, and life releasing.

WORSHIP AS LITURGY

Here we will look at worship through the lens of liturgy. *Liturgy* is a foreign word to many Protestant churches, and you may feel that this term is off-putting, unfamiliar, and cold. It may not have positive connections for you. So I want you to say it out loud five times right now and make the word less strange. Liturgy. Liturgy. Liturgy. Liturgy. Liturgy.

You may even want to say it even more times, slowly and distinctly, and pay attention to what surfaces in your consciousness. As you say or hear the word *liturgy*, what comes to mind? Gothic buildings? Lots of words printed on a page as prescribed text to be said? Juggling a hymnal, Bible, and worship book or service leaflet? Doing and saying things that don't mean much to you? Catholic and High Church practices? Incense and candles? Priests and pastors vested in strange clothing? You may be aware of other associations with the word.

Perhaps your church, or churches you have been part of, intentionally avoided any association with practices that could be called liturgical. Or you may have grown up in a church that was highly liturgical in practice, but you took the liturgy for granted or didn't understand much of what was going on. You may belong to a church you would describe as liturgical, and you deeply appreciate the liturgy as a way of shared participation in something that is a vehicle of grace in your life. Whatever your relationship to worship as liturgical activity and orientation, great riches are waiting to be discovered, even if part of the discovery is that you are not, at this point in your journey, "wired" to be a liturgical Christian!

Liturgy (Greek, *leitourgia*) derives from the synthesis of two words: *leitos*, from *leos* = *laos* (the people, the public), and *ergon* (to do, to work). Originally, *leitourgia* simply referred to "a public work" of any kind. The word did not have religious connotations. When a group of persons created a roadway or engaged in legislative action, they were acting publicly for the good of the whole community.

In a Jewish Greek translation of the Old Testament, called the Septuagint, *liturgy* referred to the sacrificial worship services in the Temple. Continuing this use, Luke 1:23 tells us Zechariah went home "when his time of service [liturgy] was ended." Hebrews 8:6 says that Jesus, the high priest of the new covenant, "has obtained a more excellent" liturgy, that is, a better kind of public religious service than that of the Temple.

Even though liturgy came to have connections to peculiarly religious actions, we need to keep in mind the more general sense of public work for the benefit of the wider community. In this book I intend for us to reflect on liturgy as it relates to justice and peace for all of humanity and the salvation of God's whole creation. In this sense, barn raisings in the nineteenth century and hurricane relief or earthquake response in the twenty-first century are liturgies. Whenever humans join in shared effort to serve the common good, that is liturgy in its broadest sense.

A small caveat: The preceding paragraph carries the risk of interpreting liturgy as a utilitarian enterprise with benefits for the participants or some larger community. That may be the nearer horizon, but on the far horizon, the liturgy of the church has one end: to know and love God and so to be one with God in God's mission. When it comes to worship, liturgy is the communal act of God's people offering themselves to the triune God in praise and prayer, using the church's historic tools and resources for the sake of the world.

These resources include holy scripture (the Bible); a calendar of celebration and a lectionary (a schedule of readings to go with the calendar); a treasury of hymns, songs, and prayers; the rites of the church centered on the sacraments of baptism and Holy Communion; and daily patterns of prayer linked to times of the day (morning, noon, evening, and night).

No Perfect Liturgy

There is no perfect or correct liturgy. There are only real, here-and-now liturgical celebrations. Books for each denomination may contain the texts and rubrics (recommended or mandatory directions) for ideal rites and rituals in its churches. However, liturgical celebration must and will always be adapted to the local context.

Further, there are degrees of liturgical observance. Some highly liturgical churches seek to observe the best ritual understandings and practices, including consistent use of the lectionary and calendar, celebration of weekly Eucharist, strong levels of participation, and much more. Others seek to worship by another scheme, including a great emphasis on worship as preaching and teaching, informal and horizontal interaction, and, sometimes, conscious rejection of what they think of as liturgy. Yet the very act of gathering for worship on the Lord's Day is a highly significant liturgical act!

In fact, churches that try not to be "liturgical" are more liturgical than they know. Even if they don't observe the Christian calendar most of the year, they do celebrate Easter and Christmas. They have an offertory, even though it is understood in purely functional terms. They read the church's book, the Bible, even if they read only a few verses from a limited number of biblical books. They baptize and observe the Lord's Supper, even if infrequently and in less-than-robust ways. So, if you attend a congregational worship service, you participate in liturgical practices to some degree.

My aim in this book is not to pigeonhole or critique any church's practice but to affirm and reflect on liturgical action and to encourage deepened participation that welcomes the fullness of the Spirit's work within us. I like to think of the church's liturgy as God's playground, with God inviting us to come out and play.

More Than Personal Devotion

Liturgy is more than personal piety. Its purpose is much deeper than commodification and distribution of religious benefits. We naturally ask, "What's in it for me?" Such self-orientation threatens and undermines the fullness of the Christian life and of the church when it focuses on, "Come to church, and we will give you what you need to live successfully." That mentality may be antiliturgy when liturgy ceases to be public work for the common good and becomes more like going to a shopping mall to buy something advertisers tell us we want or need.

The gospel names us and calls us to give up our "false selves" and to be united with our "true selves" in Jesus Christ. "Then Jesus told his disciples, 'If any want to become my followers, let them deny themselves and take up their cross and follow me. For those who want to save their life will lose it, and those who lose their life for my sake will find it'" (Matt. 16:24-25). The "self" Jesus asks us to deny is false in that it is devoted to futile ends by destructive means. The cross Jesus asks us to take up is participation in his dying and rising, an incredibly threatening and risky thought, to say the least. The prospect horrifies our false selves. To give ourselves up is impossible except by the grace of God.

This book offers an invitation to discover and participate more deeply in liturgy as God's means of uniting us with Christ in heart, mind, and work, and so, over time, to participate in God's new creation through dying and rising with Christ. Liturgy is worship for the long haul. It does not rush or give in to our fuming and insistence on our own way. It is patient and gentle. It simply goes on week by week and invites us to come along. It even carries us when our spiritual feet get tired and our energy level flags.

INFORMATION TOWARD FORMATION

While much of this book focuses on spiritual formation, I seek to balance formation with information. There are several good reasons the book needs to be informative in order for it to offer a generous invitation to more deeply formative worship practice and participation.

First, the life and the liturgy of the church have developed over millennia. Much of it has roots in the Bible and in historical and cultural settings remote from our own. For that reason I will give some background and interpretive commentary on aspects of liturgical worship so that you can appreciate and enter into them as doorways rather than as walls.

Second, liturgy and worship as *experienced* are our "primary theology." What happens in worship is our living perception of encounter with God. It is in varying degrees raw, inchoate, unexamined, unreflective, and uncritical. We simply worship without constantly taking our pulse. My intent in this book is for us to become more reflective about what we do and experience in worship as liturgy. This is "secondary theology"— reflecting on and making connections between liturgical experience and daily life experience.

I hope that an informative lens will open the door to more deeply formative participation and practice. Hopefully, what follows will open your imagination and mind to a wider and deeper appreciation of worship as intentional, communal, public prayer.

What's Ahead

I will not try to deal with all aspects of liturgical experience and practice in this small volume. Instead, I have chosen to look at some key elements of liturgy, hoping to whet your appetite for continued exploration. We will examine some central components of liturgical worship and practice. In the first chapter we will look at liturgy as patterned action and how it "works" or performs in our experience. In chapters 2 and 3, we will explore how Christians keep time with Christ through the rhythms of the day (chapter 2) and of the year (chapter 3). In the remaining chapters, we will look at the sacraments of baptism (chapter 4) and Holy Communion (chapter 5). Church history and liturgical theology will be part of these explorations, but the aim will be to attend to how the liturgy, through the power of the Holy Spirit, shapes our lives.

A Caution and a Promise

Liturgy is neither mechanical nor magical. Thinking about how liturgy shapes our lives sets us on a long journey into the realm of grace and mystery. Resist thinking, *If I go to Holy Communion once or twice, my life will be forever better and dramatically more grace filled.* That may be true, but more likely, participation in the liturgical life of the church will be a lifelong steeping in the life of God.

Enter into the liturgical life as a part of your whole spiritual journey. Open yourself to the grace of God just as you do in practices of journaling, spiritual reading, social ministry, and silence. Your personality type and where you are on your life's pathway will affect the degree to which liturgical participation will speak to you. Welcome what you can, and trust God with the rest. The church's worship has continued for over two millennia. Join in and let it carry you toward the face of God. Give yourself and your imagination to the Spirit, who breathes life into Christian public prayer. As John Wesley said in his sermon on "The Means of Grace":

> In using all means, seek God alone. In and through every outward thing look singly to the *power* of his Spirit and the *merits* of his Son. Beware you do not stick in the *work* itself; if you do, it is all lost labour. Nothing short of God can satisfy your soul. Therefore eye him in all, through all, and above all."[1]

Liturgical worship is not an end in itself. It is a portal into the heart, mind, and work of Jesus Christ by the power of the Spirit to the glory of God.

I can promise that you will meet Christ in daily prayer, in festal celebrations around the year, in the experience and remembrance of baptism, and in celebration of the Eucharist.

When Jesus talks with his disciples about how to handle fractures in the church, he concludes with this promise: "For where two or three are gathered in my name, I am there among them" (Matt. 18:20). I read that as both a promise and a yearning. The risen Christ yearns to be among us as a community of shared discipline and grace-filled worship. He promises to be present around font, book, and table. Your part is to include yourself in that community of open hands, hearts, and minds for the sake of Love.

CHAPTER 1

Liturgy as Bethel:
"This Is the Gate of Heaven"

Imagine yourself on a journey toward loving and knowing God through the liturgy of the church at worship. Imagine that others have already discovered this pathway of holiness and eagerly wait to share this journey with you. I start by telling you about one of those people. Her name was Marion.

Marion displayed a passion for ritual and the church's liturgy. A faithful soul, she would bear with "low church" worship, but if you wanted to see her light up with excitement, just don the vestments, light the incense, and use the great ritual of the church to its full measure. Then Marion would roll her eyes, press her hands together, and say, "Wonderful, wonderful. It was just glorious!" She seemed at a loss for words, almost transported by some beatific vision.

For me as a pastor seeking to plan and lead worship in the fullest, richest way I knew, she was always an encourager. When I asked the church's worship commission if we could introduce foot washing at the Holy Thursday service or if we should purchase a Paschal candle stand, Marion was altogether in favor. She was always ready to pull out all the stops with pageantry and music.

I would describe Marion as a saint and a sinner in love with Christ as she encountered him in the liturgy. Some love Christ best in silence, in compassionate service to others, or in devotional reading of scripture; but Marion loved and knew Christ best in the liturgical life of the church.

She died during Holy Week. Her funeral was held on Easter Monday. What more fitting time could there be for her friends and family to gather around Word and Table to sing and say a triumphant "alleluia" and commend her to God in the hope of the resurrection? While I could not attend, I heard that Marion's funeral was a glorious liturgy filled with laughter, love, and faith. Her grandson, who planned the service with the pastor, must have inherited her devotion to Christ in the liturgy.

What is it that Marion loved? Ultimately it was Christ, but penultimately it was the ways of worship, the experience of the community engaged in ritual, song, prayer, and praise. For Marion the communal worship of the church—its liturgy—was what Jacob called "the gate of heaven" (Gen. 28:17).

When Jacob was journeying from his home to Haran (Gen. 28:10-22), he stopped to sleep in "a certain place" (v. 11). There, with a stone for a pillow, Jacob dreamed of a ladder that reached to heaven, with God's angels ascending and descending on it. In the dream the Lord stood beside him and reiterated to him the promise God had made to Jacob's grandfather, Abraham, and his father, Isaac—promises of a land and descendants through whom all earth's peoples would find God's blessing. There, in the dream, the Lord promised Jacob the divine presence, saying, "Know that I am with you and will keep you wherever you go, and will bring you back to this land; for I will not leave you until I have done what I have promised you" (v. 15).

Then Jacob awakened and said, "'Surely the LORD is in this place—and I did not know it!' And he was afraid, and said, 'How awesome is this place! This is none other than the house of God, and this is the gate of heaven'" (vv. 16-17). Jacob got up and made a monument using his stone pillow; pouring oil on it, he called the place Bethel, the house of God.

Note Jacob's enactment of the meaning of this experience using ritual and his consecration of the place with sacred actions: setting up the stone, pouring oil, and naming the place. Jacob and Marion symbolize a host of people who know and love God in liturgical action.

GLIMPSING THE MEANING OF LITURGY

In the introduction we considered the derivation of *liturgy*, and I gave it a broad definition. Now let's consider some more specific usages of the word. In English usage, the dictionary defines *liturgy* in its primary sense: (1) all the prescribed services of the church, and (2) specifically the Eucharist. The word can also be used for the prescribed texts that order such services and as a general name for the branch of study that concerns itself with these services. *Liturgy* is commonly confused with *litany*, a specialized form of prayer. Liturgy and litany are two different things. A litany is a communal prayer in which a leader speaks a number of supplications and the congregation follows each one with a repeated response, "Lord, have mercy," for example.

For our use in this book, the dictionary definition is too narrow. I will use the term more broadly and suggest that liturgy is *patterned communal action in the worship of God*; it is *scheduled ritual actions with words.* When a congregation is doing the liturgy, it is an assembly of the faithful engaged in ordered celebration. Liturgy has to do with use of symbols and signs deeply and truthfully lived; with truth telling and honesty about the pain and tragic dimensions of life in the hope of the grace that raised Christ from the dead. The liturgy contains mystery and depth. Don Saliers hints at this when he writes, "The liturgy waits for us."[1] I invite you to play with that image as we journey together. We will return to it in later chapters.

"The liturgy waits for us!" God waits for us and for the ripening of our spirits to enter into this inheritance.

"The liturgy waits for us." Marion knew that. She knew that because it had somehow been there all along as gift and invitation. This patterned action had taken hold of her and her willingness to be drawn into the richness and risks of liturgical prayer. Not many in the congregation had been captured by it the way she had, but that was all right. "The liturgy waits for us!" God waits for us and for the ripening of our spirits to enter into this inheritance. The liturgy is there like Jacob sleeping and dreaming. When he awoke, he recognized that "this is the gate of heaven." The Spirit of God works in this patterned action with words and holy things. God waits for us week in and week out in the here-and-now gatherings of people around tangible items like water, bread, wine, oil, touch, the play of light, and the arrangement of space hallowed by prayer. The liturgy waits for you too.

In the liturgy we know God and experience God's power to shape our lives and move us from the old self to participation in the new creation. In the call-and-response pattern of the church's prayer, the Spirit disorients and reorients us, exhorting, cajoling, evoking, and provoking us into Love's service.

FORMATIVE DIMENSIONS OF LITURGY

Throughout this book we will return to reflection on the formative dimensions of the liturgy so that we can recognize God's action in forming our lives and converting us from self-preoccupation to God-referenced worship and living. Consider several ways that participation in liturgy forms us.

- *The liturgy carries us into the presence of Jesus.* Just as the friends in the Gospels carried the paralyzed man to Jesus (Luke 5:17-26), the liturgy brings us to Jesus. It breaks through the crowdedness of our preoccupations and the "false self" that keeps our true self from him. The liturgy is a means of grace. It is not something *we* do but a means through which the community called together by Christ acts in concert to bring us into the Presence. A mutual carrying takes place. In liturgical participation we carry one another into the Presence.

- *The liturgy in its repetition is cumulative yet always new.* Many hold the suspicion that liturgy as a pattern of action and words is mere repetition and therefore boring, deadly, and irrelevant. I can understand this viewpoint. Indeed, you may feel this way to some degree. I hope that our journey and your reflection on your experience will allow you to entertain a more dynamic appreciation for God's mighty and gracious action in worship as liturgy. Perhaps what seems like a stone under your head will become a pillar of recognition of how liturgy becomes the gate of heaven.

Vital liturgy requires discernment of what is "good" and "bad." In a parable Jesus speaks of casting a net. When the net is full and the fisherfolk pull it onto the shore, they put the good fish into baskets and throw away the bad ones. After telling this story, Jesus asks his followers, "Have you understood all this?" They answer, "Yes," and he says to them, "Therefore every scribe who has been trained for the kingdom of heaven is like the master of a household who brings out of his treasure what is new and what is old." (See Matthew 13:47-52.) In the recurrences of liturgical life, we learn to bring out from the treasury what is old and new, what is repetitive but ever new.

• *The liturgy is God's playground, and, by the Spirit, God calls us to "come out and play."* I mean no irreverence by describing liturgy as God's playground. Erik Erikson, the great developmental psychologist, regarded ritual activity as "ritualized play" and an essential ingredient of our spiritual being.[2] In order to develop spiritually, we need ritual play. Such play enables us to feel at home in the world and to envision how we fit into the scheme of things.

Without ritual play we are lost or exiled to the periphery and have no way to discover our story of being chosen, embraced, and called to be and belong within the immensity of the universe. In all the stages of human life, ritual play lets us find a home and a center. This play is both active and reflective. Without it we are helpless and sidelined. Without it we experience our inner and external worlds as empty and void. Ritual activity links and expands our perceptive capacities for living in a world by orienting and centering us. Imagining liturgy as God's playground can loosen us from fear that we will do something wrong or doubt that anything more than human puttering is going on. God is with us!

- *Liturgy makes us part of a web of relationships with fellow worshipers from all times and places.* When we recite the Apostles' Creed, we affirm our belief in the "communion of saints." John Wesley dismissed the various and particular saints' days as "answering no valuable end," but he dearly loved All Saints' Day as a glorious eschatological anticipation of relationship with all who have been made holy and selfless by God's grace. So the liturgy is our dancing time before God with the company of all God's people in every time and place.

  Again, the liturgy acts as a lens, allowing us to perceive gifts and relationships that are invisible in ordinary seeing. Even if we worship with a small congregation, the house is packed! Martin Luther, Julian of Norwich, Harriet Ross Tubman, Albert Schweitzer, Fanny Crosby, Mother Teresa of Calcutta, and a host of others are present too. They call us into the deeper water where we splash in the waves of God's new creation.

- *Liturgy must always reflect the catholic, or universal, dimensions of the living tradition at the same time that we make it local and particular.* Hoyt Hickman, a leader in the recovery of the historic ecumenical liturgy among United Methodists, says that if we believe in the communion of saints, then they too must have a voice in what we do around lectern, font, and table.

  Gordon Lathrop helpfully reminds us that the ordering of Christian worship (*ordo*) is best understood as a process and experience of mutual gift giving. The long and large cumulative tradition of the church universal gives us a rich and splendid gift. The Collect for Purity ("Almighty God, unto whom all hearts are open, all desires known . . .") in the Anglican and Methodist traditions, the Isaac Watts hymn "O God, Our Help in Ages Past," and the mutual act of support and blessing with which we begin liturgical prayer ("The Lord be with you, *And also with you . . .*") are examples of some of the gifts we inherit from the saints. When loved and treasured in its fullness, this legacy is also what Lathrop describes as *a remedial norm* that invites us to broaden what we tend to make exclusive, narrow, and impoverished when we limit our practices and imagination to our contemporary experience.[3]

On the other hand, the liturgy must be particular to the time and place where it happens. So, accepting the gifts that come from the larger tradition, we bring our own gifts to the table so that the legacy is always "here and now" (contemporary worship) in the fullest sense of the word. In the liturgy we receive and give gifts in ways that are venerably ancient and faithfully current.

• *Liturgy is ordered and outrageous, scheduled and uncontrollable.* This is because we are human, even when engaged in liturgical prayer. There is both grandeur and an "oh, crap" dimension to liturgical experience as a flesh-and-blood gathering around holy things. I use the phrase "oh, crap" quite literally. One Sunday morning before the second service, vested and ready, I made my way to the pulpit to see that my sermon notes were in order. People were entering the worship space. As I returned by the side aisle to take my place in the opening procession, I saw human feces on the carpet. As I recall, people were standing around, pretending not to notice! When something occurs that does not fit our perceptions or expectations, we tend to deny it. I pushed through my horror and quickly asked an usher to get the custodian to take care of the situation. I am sure that this is what happened: one of our dear saints in the early stages of dementia, with less than full consciousness of bodily functions, had experienced bowel incontinence.

Whatever our age, gender, or status, we can only gather and participate in our full humanity. For example, children participating in worship can only be themselves, sometimes to the dismay of us overly socialized adults! Would we want them to stay away? No, for we would be diminished by their absence.

In worship we are always spirits and bodies—"whole cloth"—from infancy to death. We contextualize the inherited tradition by being who and what we are. This public service to God is shaped by the realities of the truth about us and enlivened by the Holy Spirit acting in the assembly. Just as there is no perfect or correct liturgy, there are no ideal or perfect assemblies—only real local assemblies. Liturgy is not about dressing up and pretending we are other than who we are. Our quest is to give ourselves to God through this ordered prayer and so to have our affections, desires, and expressions ordered by grace and mercy.

- *The tensions inherent in the structure of the liturgy shape us.* One formative characteristic of liturgy is the way it juxtaposes one thing next to another. Don Saliers notes this when he speaks of "ambiguity" in the liturgy as a crucible in which opposites are held together, like dying to self yet being alive to God, or remaining in this world yet being a citizen of another.[4] These juxtapositions act like the tectonic plates of the earth's surface; pressure builds as one plate moves against another until a sudden release occurs. The plates shift, and pent-up energy reverberates through the adjoining regions, creating devastating newness! The earth breaks open, revealing a new situation. We experience this breaking open as destructive, but over time this process forms majestic mountain ranges. In liturgy these juxtapositions break open familiar words and actions, eventually converting and mending us. This lived liturgical experience is primary theology; it is primal and raw, even if it is mysterious and sometimes incredibly beautiful.

THE LITURGY AS ORDER (ORDO)

Now let's return to the meaning of liturgy as scheduled ritual, as patterned action with words. A common assumption is that liturgical churches use lots of words, particularly printed words. I invite you to lay aside that connection in order to embrace a broader and more dynamic appreciation of liturgy. I am indebted to Gordon Lathrop's work in *Holy Things* for the following list of patterned action and scheduled ritual. [5]

Liturgical worship is characterized by several dynamic and tensive pairings.

- *Word next to word.* In liturgical worship on the Lord's Day, guided by the lectionary (a scheduled table of Bible readings for Sundays and special days of the Christian year), we hear a reading from the Hebrew scriptures, followed by the recitation of a psalm, a reading from the Epistles, and a Gospel reading. [6] Or if we're using the daily office lectionary (a schedule of readings for daily prayer), we usually find two readings for both morning and evening prayer. [7]

One year, on vacation during Holy Week, I read the texts for Holy Thursday. The readings were from Jeremiah 20:7-11 ("O LORD, you have enticed me, and I was enticed; you have overpowered me, and you have prevailed. . . . within me there is something like a burning fire shut up in my bones; I am weary with holding it in, and I cannot.") and John 17:1-11, the prayer Jesus prays on the night before the Crucifixion, which includes the words, "For the words that you gave to me I have given to them" (v. 8). For me that day, the juxtaposition of Jeremiah next to Jesus' high priestly prayer was both fitting and ironic. In the context of the calendar, Jeremiah's words give an emotional richness to Jesus' impending passion. And in my own life the irony is that the word that we run from, the word that sets us up for trouble and difficulty, is the word that Jesus says he has "given to them"—us! Far from being Sunday-school nice, the juxtaposition of word next to word broke me open to the devastating side of this word that Jesus passes on to his beloved community. I will return to this "tectonic" moment in the next chapter.

- *Assembly next to individual.* When we participate in liturgy, we enter as individuals and become community. Western culture often glorifies and exaggerates individualism. By enacting and saying "we" and "our," the liturgy breaks open our monolithic self-referential orientation. Yet our sense of unique personhood given in Christ tempers and keeps the sense of community dynamic and ever new.

- *Seven days next to meeting on the eighth day.* Christians keep a peculiar pattern of time. We live in the seven days of creation; then on the eighth day we gather to recall the Paschal mystery—Christ's dying and rising, by which all things are being made new. (See definition of eighth day in the glossary.) We come from the week that was and take leave to the week that comes, but on the eighth day—the Lord's Day—all is gathered into Christ and made new. The juxtaposition of time next to participation in the heartbeat of Christ incorporates all of time into God's time of the eighth day. In symbolic play with this imagery, many baptismal fonts and pools are octagonal as a sign of this time that we enter in Holy Baptism.

- *Word next to Table (leading to the poor).* Another primary juxtaposition from our inheritance is the patterned celebration of proclaiming the Word of God next to the sacramental action of sharing food with one another in ways that lead to caring for the poor. Early church practice makes it clear that the tension of Word proclaimed and believed led to the table of encounter with the risen Lord, who is both guest and host (Luke 24:13-35), priest and sacrifice, and body and blood, in order to live with and in us for the sake of others. More and more churches are recovering this essential connection in ways that lead to the liturgy after the liturgy—a moral and ethical sense of being the body of Christ for the world, particularly those in greatest need. We will explore this connection further in chapter 5.

- *Praise next to lament.* Worship must be truthful. To be truthful in worship, we cannot be "happy, happy, happy," even on Easter. Suffering and tears are always present. Honest prayer finds ways to weep with those who weep. When we neglect the necessary juxtaposition of praise and lament, the liturgy becomes myopic and dishonest. The Psalms, and indeed the whole Bible, place praise and lament in proximity. For example, see Psalms 10, 13, and 22. Biblical worship maintains and enacts this dynamic interplay. The community praises God at the same time that it pleads for mercy and healing for itself and others who hurt and suffer. As we will see in chapter 2, the Psalms are our school of prayer in ways that help us find our voice to sing in both major and minor keys.

- *Teaching leading to baptism (as full initiation into the sacraments and the community of faith).* In the latter half of the twentieth century, Christians began to recover and implement the vital connection between formation and baptism as practiced by the church since the second century. Baptism as initiation into Christ and into the church can never be a mere moment in time; it requires of us a journey with those God is drawing into a shared life in Christ. The rite of baptism assumes that relationships have been created between those seeking and the church. It assumes that these relationships will continue on the other side of the bath. We will explore this idea further in chapter 4.

- *Year next to the Easter mystery.* What the eighth day is to the week, Easter is to the year. Easter is the hinge for the Christian sense of time. Symbolically and sometimes quite literally, Christians enter into union with Christ in his dying and rising (Rom. 6:3-11), at a primordial service called the Easter Vigil. This first service of Easter in which candidates are baptized connects us to Christ, our Passover Lamb. The days from evening on Holy Thursday through Easter mark our passage from death to life, from slavery to freedom, from sin to righteousness, from blindness to illumination. In this liturgical passage all time and events are changed, both their significance and their power to determine our actions and thinking. Though we continue to live our lives in calendar time (*chronos*), we are made part of God's new creation (2 Cor. 5:17)—joined to Christ, the firstborn from the dead (Col. 1:18) and our future (1 Cor. 15:20-28).

• *Ancient things next to the New Hope.* The hubris of our age evidences itself in our glorification of all things contemporary and dismissal of the viewpoints of antiquity and other cultures. When my wife and I married at age twenty, my grandmother offered to buy us silverware. We said we would rather have modern Danish stainless steel!

Liturgy embraces the tectonic plate of tradition pressing against the unfolding hope of the gospel. Leonard Sweet, Robert Webber, and others have made "ancient-future" a common word for an emerging appreciation of the creative juxtaposition of past, present, and future. Liturgy knows that the canon of biblical words and the ancient practices of the church shape our parochial and narrowed contemporary vision.

In faithful liturgical life we also know that sermons and new songs and stories connect and interpret the tradition for this time and place in which we live. Part of the reform and renewal of the Roman Catholic Church since Vatican II is the recovery of profound biblical scholarship and preaching that connects the ancient things to the yearnings and hopes of present-day people.

These are some of the central features of what we mean by the liturgy as patterned communal actions and scheduled ritual with words. This gives us some handholds for our rock climb of exploring the rhythms and formative dimensions of the liturgy. These conceptual frames offer structure to our conversation. Though they are important, it is just as important to remember Marion loving God in the liturgy and pressing her hands together and exclaiming, "Wonderful, wonderful! It was just glorious." In worship we are there—in the house of God, with angels ascending and descending. That is primary experience shaping us for living in Love's service. Reflection on the experience is critical but secondary. Like a gardener eating a just-picked ripe tomato, the delight is in the experience. In reflection the gardener considers all that preceded the picking and how to do it better next season. In our conversation together, we will reflect on our experience and how it conforms us to Christ.

REFLECTING ON YOUR EXPERIENCE OF LITURGY

Recall your experience of holy things, holy people, holy days, and holy actions from your childhood experience of liturgy in church and home. Now reflect on your current experience of holy things, holy people, holy places, holy patterning of time, and holy actions. Have there been experiences and moments when, with Jacob, you could say, "Surely the LORD is in this place—and I did not know it!"?

How has your experience of liturgy shaped your life and your identity as a Christian? In what ways has communal worship been "the gate of heaven" for you? If several ideas come to mind, list them, then brood more deeply as time and energy allow.

PRAYER FOR A TIME
OF REFLECTION

God, awesome in presence and power,
    there are many times and situations
    where I have not known
    that you were there
    until later.

I come to the scriptures in the morning,
    and I am sleepy.
I come to the Communion table
    to receive bread and cup;
I sense no mystery,
    and I fail to discern that I belong to a community.
I come to the shadows of the evening,
    only to keep going with my work.
I meet a homeless person asking for help,
    and I don't realize that I am standing
    in the house of God.

Come stand beside me
    in this time of listening and learning.
Give me new eyes to see liturgy
    as none other than the house of God
    and the gate of heaven
    through Christ our Lord.
Amen.

CHAPTER 2

Daily Prayer with the Church: The Daily Office

You may have grown up in a neighborhood where a church bell tolled the hours of the day. Or perhaps you now live in a setting where you hear a church bell ring on Sunday morning, calling all who hear it to come and worship.

I remember as a child the excitement of being chosen to ring the bell before worship. Though I did not understand the long tradition of ringing the bell, I delighted in taking hold of the thick hemp rope and pulling down with all my might to get the bell to turn and make the clapper strike the rim of the big bell in the tower. For me it was an opportunity to "throw my weight around" and make a noise that people could hear all around the village. For the church, it was a call to prayer and worship. If you have been to Taizé, the ecumenical community in France, you know the thrill of hearing the bells call everyone in that place to prayer in the morning, at midday, and at evening.

The tolling of the bell serves as a call to worship, a call to the deepest part of us to stop our occupations, whether leisure or work, and attend to God. Though this practice has faded in many parts of the world, it persists in some places as a reminder of the importance of keeping time with Christ.

Ordering Time and Communal Prayer

Drawing upon our Jewish inheritance, many Christians seek to keep holy time. We mark time and punctuate it with recollections of God-with-us as a way of hallowing all time. Even the least liturgical churches observe cycles of time. For example, with few exceptions, Christians worship on the Lord's Day as the eighth day, the day God raised Jesus from the dead. Most denominations encourage their members to take time at the start of each day to read the Bible, reflect on the connections of God's mercy and the day ahead, and pray. Many churches distribute a daily devotional guide such as *The Upper Room*, which includes a suggested scripture reading, meditation, and prayer for the day.

Our inheritance of keeping time with Christ focuses primarily around the cycles of the *day* (sunrise, zenith, sunset, and night), the *week* (Monday to Saturday next to Sunday), and the *year* (the springtime Passover and the winter solstice). As we noted in the last chapter, these juxtapositions of one thing next to another are part of the ordering (*ordo*) of Christian worship.

We will explore the calendar of the year in the next chapter. Here we will explore the rhythm of daily prayer as an ancient and contemporary practice that shapes our lives in communion with the church around the world.

Daily Prayer

Our inheritance of liturgical daily prayer has roots in the Bible and ancient practices of the Jewish people. Jewish liturgical prayer coincided with the hours of temple sacrifice: morning (Ps. 5:3; 59:16; 88:13; 92:2) and evening (1 Kings 18:36; Ezra 9:5; Ps. 141:2; Dan. 9:21) oblations were the usual times. Psalm 55:17 and Daniel 6:10 suggest that prayer three times a day was recognized as especially appropriate. Psalm 119:164 ("Seven times a day I praise you for your righteous ordinances") supports the monastic practice of praying the daily offices to mark seven periods of the day.

Christians have continued this practice of prayer connected to the times of the day. The Roman Catholic tradition calls this daily cycle the *liturgy of the hours*. The orthodox tradition calls it the *divine office*. The Episcopal Church's Book of Common Prayer calls it the *daily office*. United Methodists call it *daily praise and prayer*, including services for morning, midday, evening, and night. The Presbyterian *Book of Common Worship* provides the people with services titled Morning Prayer, Midday Prayer, Evening Prayer, and Prayer at the Close of Day. In all of these traditions we find a marking of time for the four "seasons" of the day: sunrise, heat of the day, cool of the day, and night. Whatever we call it, it is punctuating the hours of the day with ritual prayer. It is sanctifying the hours: "Watch and pray, that you may not enter into temptation" (Mark 14:38, WEB).

This watching and waiting keeps faith, hope, and love alive; anticipates Christ's coming at an hour we do not know; and shapes our prayer within a larger communal context. In the process we live out our Lord's Day "sacrifice, in union with Christ's offering for us"[1] in the full range of daily life. While the ancient church held to the evangelical ideal of praying without ceasing (1 Thess. 5:17), they found that prayer (*ora*) at assigned hours shaped, deepened, and focused their unceasing prayer during work (*labora*) and all that surrounded it. I can witness to the gift of the discipline of ceasing from work or whatever I am doing to light the evening candle and join in the church's prayer. I can also witness to how often I fail to cease work to participate in the church's prayer. As with all of our discipleship, daily prayer is a practice acquired with persistence, even when we fail.

DAILY PRAYER WITH THE CHURCH OR PRIVATE DEVOTIONS?

If we go to a monastic community and share in its prayer and worship for a day or a week, we will experience the rhythm of the daily office as communal prayer. The daily office is quite different from solitary prayer or "daily devotions." When we enter into communal prayer at sunrise, midday, sunset, and bedtime, we get a different sense of our roots and our connections to God and the life of the world. Communal prayer goes on around the world through all the hours of the day. As earth turns into the light of sunrise and then into darkness, we join with monastic communities, cathedral choirs, priests and pastors ringing the bell and praying the daily office alone or with those who join them, with laymen and women who gather their household members to join in hymn and psalm. This liturgical prayer occurs in every time zone day by day by day.

The recovery of the discipline of daily prayer is a major component of liturgical renewal in the church. All of the ecumenical Christian traditions encourage liturgical prayer by providing ritual texts for these services. In practice, daily prayer has yet to gain significant recovery among the faithful. Here again the liturgy waits for us. For many of us, the emotional connections to this practice are our childhood and youth experiences of vespers at summer camp or the tradition of holy songs around the campfire. Increasing numbers of adult Christians from the less liturgical traditions are discovering the blessing of being able to share in the life of a monastic community for a day or more and learning about the richness of communal daily prayer. This sense of time and community tends to continue in daily life when they leave the monastery.

Part of the gift of the daily office and occasional immersions in its practice is the discovery that even when we pray alone, we are not alone. Rather, others are praying with and for us. Resources are available that help to affirm and actualize this communal sense.[2] In using a form and prayers that others also are using, we connect to a larger concert of praise and prayer. Use of the daily office with a lectionary of readings allows us to participate in *common prayer*. With others we recite the Psalms, read scriptures, and offer prayer for the church, the world, and all who suffer. This practice enculturates a sense of solidarity among all the baptized as a priestly community before God. It also draws us into the life and heart of God.

THE ROOTS OF DAILY PRAYER

In the Old Testament (Hebrew Bible), the practice of saying prayers at fixed hours of the day was general among the Jews. Even if praying seven times a day was an ideal, it is reasonable to assume that those who sought to practice their faith would pray at primary times of the day: sunrise, midday, sunset, and bedtime.

The New Testament (Greek Bible) gives this description of the new church's life together: "They devoted themselves to the apostles' teaching and fellowship, to the breaking of bread and the prayers" (Acts 2:42). No New Testament references indicate the form of these prayers. The scriptures allude to the times of prayer (Acts 10:9—noon; Acts 12:5, 12—night; Acts 16:25—midnight), but it is impossible to know whether these were set times for prayer in the early Christian community. We can reasonably assume that because these first Christians were embedded in a Jewish matrix, they practiced prayer as they had known it in synagogue and home. So they probably prayed at least in the morning and evening prayer times.

The monastics of Syria, Egypt, and Gaul were the first to organize a complete daily office, including recitation of the whole Psalter, set times for "reunion" (communal prayer in the round of monastic solitude), and set patterns for prayer. In cathedrals and parish churches, a simpler form of the daily office developed, consisting of morning and evening prayers.

In the late fifth century, monastic communities began to observe ritual prayer seven times a day. Here is a list of the names of those services and the time of day for each:

> Nocturns (before daybreak)
> Prime (6:00 a.m.)
> Terce (9:00 a.m.)
> Sext (midday)
> None (3:00 p.m.)
> Vespers (6:00 p.m.)
> Compline (before retiring for bed)

Notice that the services occurred at roughly three-hour intervals. There was also a nighttime office of vigils called Matins, or the office of readings. Saint Benedict is credited with fixing the detail of the services in his Rule; he named it "the work of God" (*Opus Dei*) in the rhythm of prayer and work (*ora et labora*).

Keeping the office became obligatory for clergy during the Middle Ages, and *breviaries* became common as a way of making available the Psalms, antiphons, hymns, lessons, responses, versicles, and prayers in a convenient package or compendium. This saved those praying the divine office from having to use several books. The tradition of chant (Latin, Gregorian, English) grew up around the divine office. The Reformation, especially in the English church, led to a reduction of the divine office to two services: morning and evening prayer (Matins and Evensong). In 1971, Vatican II reforms led to a radical rearrangement of the offices and a new title: liturgy of the hours.

All of the services in the daily office seem to have taken psalmody combined with scripture readings followed by prayers as the basic pattern. So the essential flow of the morning and evening services included the act of gathering and praise using a canticle, chanting or recitation of psalms, scripture readings followed by canticle or canticles, and prayers, including the Lord's Prayer. Canticles are songs from the Bible (for example, the Song of Zechariah and the Song of Mary, both from Luke 1) or historic use (such as the Te Deum or the Gloria in Excelsis). Here is the outline for Evening Prayer and Morning Prayer:

Evening Prayer	*Morning Prayer*
Opening responsories	Opening responsories
(lucernarium: lighting the	Psalmody
evening lamp)	Scripture lessons with
Psalmody	canticles/commentaries/
Scripture lessons with	spiritual readings
canticles/commentaries/	Prayers
spiritual readings[3]	
Prayers	

One last note on the background of the church's daily office: its form took different shape depending on its context.

In the desert, where monks in community gave all their time to prayer, the daily office multiplied to seven times a day, plus the *nocturns*. This is called the *monastic pattern of daily prayer*. In urban settings the daily office took a simpler form, consisting of public morning and evening prayer called the *cathedral office*. The cathedral office emphasized praise and prayer rather than systematic recitation of the Psalter and ordered reading of the Bible.

As mentioned previously, recent prayer books reflect these varied traditions. Most monastic communities, true to their heritage, have updated breviaries that discipline them to recite the whole Psalter every week, along with a course of readings from scriptures and commentary from saints and doctors of the church. On the other extreme, we find a deliberate attempt to revive the cathedral office in "Daily Praise and Prayer" services in *The United Methodist Book of Worship* and *The United Methodist Hymnal*. These brief, simple services focus on praise to God and intercession for the world. There is no attempt to recite the whole Psalter or read the scriptures in course. These services are composed of two principal elements: hymns and psalms of praise, and prayers of intercession for the world and the church.

In the middle between these extremes are the approaches taken in the Book of Common Prayer, *The Lutheran Book of Worship*, and *The Book of Common Worship*. In those resources you find a compromise between disciplined recitation of Psalter and scripture on the one hand, and simplicity and brevity on the other. The Order of Saint Luke has also taken this approach in its six volumes, *The Daily Office*.

As we pray the daily office, we make rich and natural connections with the time of day. In Morning Prayer we welcome the new day and anticipate the new creation breaking into our relationships and work. Morning Prayer also recalls the creation narrative when God created the light and called it day (Gen. 1:1-5). Christologically, the rising sun resonates with our affirmation of Christ's victory over the powers of darkness and death. We anticipate the day, ask God for guidance in the tasks that lie before us, and give ourselves to sharing in God's love, which encompasses the world and the church with mercy and grace.

At the sun's zenith we pause for Midday Prayer to welcome a respite from the day's work and seek the replenishing of our strength, acknowledging that our strength comes from the Lord. This office is shorter and simpler than Morning Prayer or Evening Prayer. In this office we thank God for the midday time of rest, ask God to bless the work we have begun, and invite God to perfect it so that it pleases God. In Midday Prayer we also connect to the Paschal narrative, remembering that at this hour Jesus hung on the cross, and darkness came over the land (Mark 15:33). We recognize afresh the self-giving of God, who in Christ stretched out arms of love on the hard wood of the cross. In response to this cruciform love, we recommit ourselves to take up Love's cross in our moral and ethical responsibilities and relationships.

At the setting of the sun, we cease our work and pray Evensong (another name for Evening Prayer). In this office we accept the lengthening shadows and daylight's fading. With all people of every time and place who met the coming darkness by lighting lamps, we light a single candle or lamp (a connection with the Paschal mystery and Easter). In this service we step away from the day's activities to again give ourselves to prayer, anticipating rest from our labor and a night of sleep, and committing ourselves to God's protection. We also sing or recite Mary's song as a declaration of God's ongoing work of mercy and justice:

> My soul magnifies the Lord,
>   and my spirit rejoices in God my Savior,
> for he has looked with favor on the lowliness
>   of his servant.
> Surely, from now on all generations
>   will call me blessed;
> for the Mighty One has done great things for me,
>   and holy is his name.
> His mercy is for those who fear him
>   from generation to generation.
> He has shown strength with his arm;
>   he has scattered the proud in
>   the thoughts of their hearts.
> He has brought down the powerful from their thrones,
>   and lifted up the lowly;
> he has filled the hungry with good things,
>   and sent the rich away empty.
> He has helped his servant Israel,
>   in remembrance of his mercy,
>   according to the promise he made to our ancestors,
>   to Abraham and to his descendants forever.
>   (Luke 1:46-55)

At the close of the day, bedtime, we pray Night Prayer, or Compline. We accept the end of the day and rehearse the final yielding of ourselves to God. You may remember being taught to pray this bedtime prayer:

Now I lay me down to sleep.
I pray the Lord my soul to keep.
If I should die before I wake,
I pray the Lord my soul to take.[4]

This prayer illustrates the spirit of Night Prayer as a "little dying" at the end of the day. Night Prayer includes singing or reciting Simeon's song upon seeing the infant Jesus:

Now, Lord, you let your servant go in peace;
    your word has been fulfilled.
My own eyes have seen the salvation
    which you have prepared in the sight of every people:
    a light to reveal you to the nations
    and the glory of your people Israel.
                      (Luke 2:29-32)[5]

With this old man we practice coming to the end, commending our souls and bodies to God, and affirming the hope of a new day and the resurrection of the dead.

How Daily Prayer Relates to Worship on the Lord's Day

While the Lord's Day service of Word and Table proclaims and enacts the gospel, daily prayer lives into and out of the good news embodied in preaching and sacrament on the Lord's Day. Daily prayer enables the church to "abide in," "remain in," and attend to the risen Christ through the hours of the day and the days of the week (John 15:1-17). This is the rhythm of week next to Sunday; it is part of the *ordo* we looked at in chapter 1. The daily office invites us to live the liturgy more deeply.

Liturgical prayer as known in the daily office draws us into rich practices of prayer: praying the Psalms, praying other scriptures, praying lived experience, praying the silence, and praying with the saints.

Praying the Psalms

The Psalter is the foundation of the daily office and has proved to be the Christian's school of prayer. Thomas Merton wrote, "We must go on plunging our leprosy, like Naaman, in this Jordan, this stream of Psalmody."[6] Merton's comment about Naaman (see 2 Kings 5 for the story) gets at the depth of what transpires over a long, prayerful soak in the language of these ancient songs, hymns, laments, coronation texts, and wisdom prayers. In this ongoing plunge we find healing and wholeness.

In the Psalms we journey with the human family at full stretch. These scriptures call us to allow the whole range of our emotions, conflicts, and wonderment to have their moment on the stage. Walter Brueggemann broadly categorizes the Psalms as mad, glad, and sad. In the Psalms we experience the world's and our own orientation, disorientation, and reorientation. The Psalter is the urtext (original text) of Jewish and Christian prayer. As I continue to pray the Psalms, I recognize again and again how the liturgy has been shaped, formed, and given its vocabulary by the Psalter.

The Psalms provide medicine for the anemia of our prayers. They are not M&M's but iron pills! In them you find robust expressions of agony, suffering, ecstatic praise, hatred, and longing for revenge. And most delightfully, the Psalms can and should be sung, even if you pray them in solitude and in distant company with the church. Spend some time with a monastic community that sings them, and you will think you have come home to the house of prayer. The haunting memory of psalmody will linger in your mind and spirit. The Benedictine monastery near my home sometimes chants the Psalms on a single tone while the accompanist offers chordal support. When I worked at the General Board of Discipleship, I loved to sing the Psalms in the men's room or in the stairwells of the Denman Building where I worked because of the incredibly good acoustics in those places. The sound echoed and surrounded me as if I were singing in an ancient stone church.

Praying the Psalms lets us discover our humanity in the words of Jews and Christians before us. In them we find the grace to *be*. In my journal for May 9, 2003, I mused:

> Just now I realized in a fleeting way that one way to read the Psalms is to enter into the experience of the words—that is, to pray the psalm as if all that is being asserted is true for me; as if what the psalmist pleads for is out of *my* plight, *my* delight, *my* yearning. This is in contrast to reading the Psalms with some distance, as if I'm not identified with the experience and perception of the psalmist.

Praying the Psalms as corporate prayer, we are one with the church and the whole human family: these are our prayers in concert with the yearnings of the world. There is much more to praying the Psalms. I urge you to read some of the works of classic and contemporary spiritual writers such as Dietrich Bonhoeffer, C. S. Lewis, and Thomas Merton.

Praying the Scriptures
Devotional reading of the Bible, or *lectio divina*, differs from the reading we learned to do in school. Rather than reading for

information, challenge, or simply to get through a text, *lectio divina* involves the guidance of the Holy Spirit. This prayerful, attentive reading of the scriptures using a daily lectionary (different from a Sunday lectionary) calls us to a systematic reading of scripture.[7]

In communal settings, silence after the reading and a time of contemplation after daily prayer permit the texts to speak to us. When praying the office alone, allow time for extended brooding and journaling on the reading(s). Sometimes you may read until a word or phrase calls for you to stop and live into the epiphany of God. Here is one such moment as I noted it in my journal based on the two lectionary readings for that day:

Morning Prayer—Holy Thursday, April 7, 2003

Jeremiah 20:7-11: The word of the Lord fascinates and entices. But be careful. It may be your ruin. The reading for this day connects with the urgency of Jesus' situation. Embody the word, and it will take you out into the mystery that is death, or you must shrink from it. The text explores the complex relationship between God and the prophet. The prophet does own his part in the relationship. "I was enticed." I let this happen. I paid attention. I kept responding as you led me along.

John 17:1-11: "For the words that you gave to me I have given to them" (v. 8). The word that dupes, entices, fascinates, destroys, and gives life gets passed on! No wonder people are wary of getting in with this crowd around the Word. No wonder they fear for their children to be baptized into this Word and water. It drowns, kills, takes you to the cross. No wonder we are tempted to turn away from this Word and be done with its resounding in our hearts and minds. And no wonder we return to it, cling to the Word, give image to it, and tell its story in Triduum [the three days between Holy Thursday and Easter evening] rituals so we see its fullness as the ways of death and life, cross and empty tomb, agonizing and ecstasy. "Now they know . . . ," says Jesus. There is this "pass it on" thing in the gospel of Jesus. The Word received is handed on—tradition [*traditio* = handing on]. This is how "we" make disciples, how we are continually re-formed as disciples.

Praying Lived Experience

In praying the Psalms and the scriptures, we have a new context for the concerns of the moment—our own and those of the suffering, the world, and the church. Here there is gift and freedom to use the great liturgical prayer forms of the church, including extemporaneous prayer in thanksgiving, intercession, penitence, and supplication. Sometimes we need to be carried in this venture of formation in Christ. The ancient and modern prayers of the church do just that as we make them our own. At other times we have a kind of charismatic energy that bursts forth with the fire of words formed in the crucible of our hearts and minds.

Sometimes a prayer text or another spiritual reading launches us into expression that seems to well up within us. In my journal for May 20, 2003, I journaled after walking the Chelsea Pier in New York City and having read a section in Thomas Moore's *Original Self: Living with Paradox and Originality*. I prayed in my journal:

God of all creation,
>   we wonder at what you have made,
>   like the frog that croaks,
>   "How you made me jump!"

It is not our perfection that causes us to wonder,
>for we only speak of perfection
>when we see a newborn child.
Within days the patina begins to fade,
>and each of us joins the neurotic human race—
>crying, anxious,
>making power plays
>to conceal our insecurity and fear.
Creation is real—not ideal.
Creation is your invitation
>to partnership over the long haul—
>a journey in compassion
>toward ourselves and toward others
>who share with us
>the same imperfections and insecurities—
>the raw material that your active grace
>must love and shape all our days.

Praying the Silence

In her introduction to *Amazing Grace: A Vocabulary of Faith*, Kathleen Norris tells about her experiences of attending worship services after years of being away from the church. The words were inaccessible to her, like meaningless code words assaulting her. She describes feeling exhausted after worship and needing three-hour naps. Then she stumbled across a Benedictine monastery where wonderful times of silence followed readings or psalms. She found the experience of worship and words much more accessible. The monks were less anxious to fill the air with words. They allowed for silence so they had time to digest the words spoken and read. Norris experienced this rhythm of words and silence as blessing, gift, and refreshment. So for us in praying the daily office, we pray well when we enter into the spaces between the words and allow the inner light of the Spirit to make the Psalms, scriptures, and prayers shine with truth and glory.

Silences in the daily office, like rests in music, are essential to the overall experience. Without silences to rest, reflect, and internalize the gifts from the Spirit, we simply pile up words like a glut of presents on Christmas morning. Without silences, the readings and prayers are hindered from shaping our lives in holiness.

Praying with the Saints

We need holy exemplars. The communion of the saints can be more than just a doctrine as we imaginatively entertain the saints' stories and presence among the heavenly host. This creative recollection can become a portal into a richly textured sense of communion with those who have lived and died well. The church through the ages has developed a calendar of remembrance called the *sanctoral cycle*, in distinction to the seasons of the Christian year or liturgical cycle. You can find a particular rendering of the sanctoral cycle in the Book of Common Prayer under "Holy Days." For more ample biographical sketches of bishops, martyrs, teachers, musicians, and other holy men and women, see *Lesser Feasts and Fasts* (Episcopal) and *For All the Saints: A Calendar of Commemorations for United Methodists*.[8]

I delight in praying the daily office in company with Charles Wesley, Mary Magdalene, Polycarp, John Donne, Catherine of Siena, Julian of Norwich, and many more. Their persistence in holy practices encourages me, and they remind me that God did not stop raising up great holy men and women with the close of the New Testament. They prompt me to believe in what God seeks to do in changing me from sinner to saint. If they lived out their baptism in daily life, then so can we! In living with and praying with the saints, our sense of the communion of saints becomes a rich treasury of stories and a participation in a community of the living and the dead.

Praying the Environment and Time

As suggested previously, praying the daily office heeds the connections to the time of day. Morning Prayer invites us to attend to the ever-varying natural light of each new day. Some days are bright, others cloudy. The light of the new day around the winter solstice differs from morning light around the summer solstice. When we pray in tune with natural light, Morning Prayer breaks the sameness of artificial electric light, and God plays with our spirits. Similarly, the setting of the sun brings changing light, and the light of a candle invites observance and attentiveness to the fading of day for Evening Prayer. Sometimes I find attentiveness to light to be the most significant aspect of Evening Prayer. When I am at home, an icon illuminated by a candle cultivates a deeper attentiveness to the One who is present to welcome our prayers and praises. Again, words have a rich context in which to take hold of my mind, heart, and affections. I can imagine the lighting of a single candle or oil lamp in other places where Christians' Evening Prayer precedes, follows, or coincides with my offering of praise and prayer. I carry a small paper icon and a small, flat candle with me when traveling so I can set up a movable oratory wherever I go.

During one recent Holy Week, my wife and I celebrated our fortieth anniversary in Hawaii. I prayed the daily office looking out over the Pacific as it rolled toward me each morning and evening. Praying the office in that setting was more leisurely than normal weekdays afforded. I journaled a lot in those days. On Easter Tuesday, I wrote:

I am realizing again this morning that in praying the daily office, as in the use of the other means of grace, we sow faithfully that we may harvest richly. There are not so much immediate results of this practice as there is a long-term cultivation of both an orientation and a cumulative investment in words, phrases, and reflections that build a huge network of connections for the heart and mind. There is little instant gratification here, and, sadly, few Christians persist in this or ever start. It is easier to act like bees flitting from one spiritual flower to the next without praying the same prayer twice or regularly and consistently attending to the full range of the scriptures in light of the Christian year. There is great wisdom built into the daily office that invites an athlete of the Spirit to run this course and to train in this way over a lifetime.

Getting Started

While I hope that what you have already read offers practical possibilities, I want to offer some specific approaches for beginning the practice of the daily office as a discipline of prayer with the church.

- *Get a useful and workable daily prayer book.* A number of books contain the resources you need to pray the daily office: the Book of Common Prayer; *Book of Common Worship, Daily Prayer; A Guide to Prayer for Ministers and Other Servants;* the Order of Saint Luke's *Daily Office;* and a number of online sources.[9] I have used several of these, but the convenience of the Book of Common Prayer has been my home base. What works for you may be as simple as a card or as complex as a multivolume daily office. The structure and text need to be something you resonate with and can work with in the time you can devote to the daily office. For resources, see the bibliography (p. 155).

- *Consider making daily prayer a communal experience in your church, home, or office.* Over a twelve-year period as a pastor, I prayed Morning Prayer at an announced time at church on weekdays and published it in the church newsletter. People knew I would be there and they were welcome to come. Some came occasionally. One man, Bob, came for five years daily, even when I could not be there. We prayed the Psalms, took turns reading the weekday lectionary readings, and made intercession for others.

- *Create a space—an oratory—for praying the daily office.* Environment is important. Create a space where you can pray or sing aloud, even if only in a whisper. Remember, the daily office is vocal and visible participation with the ecumenical community of prayer. Your space can be fixed or movable, depending on your lifestyle. Your dining table or a corner of a room will do. At church, use the sanctuary or a chapel if available. If you will pray the daily office with others, get the needed books (prayer books, Bibles, hymnals, etc.) so others can participate fully. Have available matches and a candle, especially for Evening Prayer. If this space is at home, set up a small table and place a candle, icon, or some other object on it to give the space a focal point. Use a shelf or other surface for your Bible, daily office book, hymnal, journal, prayer list, and other resources.

- *Be bold and sing the parts of the service that you can.* Sing or chant the Psalms to a simple tone. Sing the canticles and hymns. You can find psalm tones in *The United Methodist Hymnal* (p. 737), in the *Book of Common Worship, Daily*

Prayer (pp. 170–79 with instructions on p. 169), and in other sources. If you are not a singer, don't let this suggestion discourage you; recitation of the psalms and canticles is a faithful practice. Make the best music your heart and head can offer to God.

- *Learn to pray the office by spending time with a monastic community.* I suggest this so that the rhythms of prayer at sunrise, zenith, sunset, and night get into your psyche and spirit. You will find that immersion in communal daily prayer orients you and takes root in your life in ways you continue at home.

- *Pray parts of the office at their proper times, even if you are actively engaged in work and ministry.* I pray parts of the four daily services while climbing stairs, sitting on the toilet, driving, or pulling the covers up to my neck at day's end. If weariness makes praying all of Night Prayer impractical, I sometimes simply recite "Our help is in the name of the Lord, the maker of heaven and earth" and then say the Song of Simeon (Luke 2:29-32) or sing "Into your hands, O Lord, I commend my spirit" (see Ps. 31:5). Or at sunset, I walk along the beach and pray the parts of Evening Prayer I can remember, along with intercessions for all in need, the earth, the church, and the world. In all of this, I know that I am carried by and participate with the church, whose "voice of prayer is never silent."[10]

QUESTIONS FOR REFLECTION

1. How has the discipline of daily prayer—whether personal private prayer or some form of the daily office—shaped your life?

2. What obstacles loom before you as you think of praying the daily office consistently? What could you do to address those obstacles?

3. In what ways do you feel called to this practice?

4. As you imagine praying the daily office, whom might you invite to join you in this discipline? Listen to the Holy Spirit's promptings.

CHAPTER 3

Cycles in Time:
The Christian Year and Spirituality

O love, how deep, how broad, how high,
it fills the heart with ecstasy,
that God, the Son of God, should take
our mortal form for mortals' sake!

For us baptized, for us he bore
his holy fast and hungered sore,
for us temptation sharp he knew;
for us the tempter overthrew.

For us he prayed; for us he taught;
for us his daily works he wrought;
by words and signs and actions thus
still seeking not himself, but us.

For us to evil power betrayed,
scourged, mocked, in purple robe arrayed,
he bore the shameful cross and death,
for us gave up his dying breath.

For us he rose from death again;
for us he went on high to reign;
for us he sent his Spirit here,
to guide, to strengthen, and to cheer.

All glory to our Lord and God
for love so deep, so high, so broad:
the Trinity whom we adore,
forever and forevermore.[1]

This hymn focuses on God's action for us in a praise-filled narrative that helps us sense our location in God's world and in the love of the triune God. In six short stanzas it recounts the whole work of Christ Jesus, a story the liturgy takes a full year to tell. The liturgical structures of time and ritual play invite us to experience anew an ever-deepening sense of our place in God's story. When we worship God in the context of the liturgy, the Holy Spirit gives us an awesome and awe-inspiring challenge of telling the story of what God has done.

We could compare the ongoing experience of worship to backpacking with a topographical map—we explore the depth, height, and breadth of God's love. In corporate worship we rehearse and experience the contours of a love that reveals our identity, gives us our vocation and sustains us in it, weaves us into a community gathered around the risen Christ, locates us in time and space, holds us accountable for living responsibly, and guides us on the journey, even when it becomes extreme in agonizing ethical choices, sickness, or death.

In this chapter we will explore and interpret the formative dimensions of the way Christians keep time with the risen Christ. The Christian calendar of celebration takes into account the past, present, and future in order to help us form and be formed in ways of seeing and patterns of living God's pilgrimage with the cosmos. This calendar of observance shapes our attitudes toward all time. It enables us to deal with the tensions of living between morning and evening, between last Sunday and this Sunday, between last Easter and next Easter, and between Christ's first and future advents.

Liturgical worship glories in and relishes the story of Jesus in ways that are amazingly simple and deceptively complex.

The church's liturgy gains its distinctive way of telling God's story by using a calendar and a related table of scripture readings called a *lectionary*. Without this calendar Christian worship would be quite different, as it is in churches that follow some other plan of varying the pace and focus of telling the good news. Liturgical worship glories in and relishes the story of Jesus in ways that are amazingly simple and deceptively complex. And best of all, this way of "playing" on God's turf is life transforming, or it can be, if we act as if it really matters. And it does!

A colleague once asked me, "Why do people come up to you just before you enter the sanctuary to lead worship and urgently tell you about some detail in their lives or someone else's? For example, a trustee tells you that the church's lawn mower is on the fritz, or a parishioner says she is going to vacation in Borneo for a month. Why do they do that, when it seems totally out of context just as you are about to process down the aisle?"

Then he answered his own question: "Maybe it's because somehow they know that we all could go into worship and be forever changed! God's presence and power just might make us forget all of the silly, mundane facts of our lives and take us out into the deep where God's mission and love sweep us into God's own passion for the world."

For all the hyperbole of his query and answer, I think my colleague was exactly right. The liturgy is just that: momentous and dangerous. It's just that messy and potent. How tragic that we act as if nothing is at stake and yawn as we open our hymnals to sing the first hymn!

Now let's consider how the calendar of Christian worship developed as an annual cycle of immersing us in God's story Sunday by Sunday and season by season. God calls us to come and play on God's turf and in God's time. That is what the calendar and lectionary are about. In liturgy we join in the play.

THE STORY OF OUR CHRISTIAN CALENDAR

The gospel of Jesus Christ structures how Christians observe and experience time. The calendar of the Christian year did not exist from the beginning. You will not find it laid out in the New Testament as "the Christian calendar" or "Thus says the Lord, 'Here is how you shall organize the Lord's Days.'" Perhaps that fact troubles you and makes you feel that the calendar is an additional layer of tradition beyond what is scriptural. In one sense that is true. Yet, if we believe that the Holy Spirit has worked and still works to form a community of grace around Jesus and the story of God's love for us, then we can trust that the Spirit has spun out a playful way of telling the story of the height, depth, and breadth of the love of God that continually calls us to find ourselves in God's creating and redeeming tale. Since God has not yet finished playing with us, the story of the calendar is still evolving.[2]

So here in brief is how the yearly cycle of telling the story came to be. As the ancient missionary church moved out from its Jewish origins at the eastern end of the Mediterranean Sea, it found a way (perhaps stumbled over the Holy Spirit's unseen foot) to tell the gospel story and to form people in light of God's defeat of evil and death. The church's outreach to and inclusion of pagan people who had no formation in the Jewish Bible and ethos required some manner of rehearsing and celebrating the life-transforming good news of Jesus Christ. Over several hundred years, Christians found the shape of the Paschal mystery (the passion, death, and resurrection of Christ Jesus) mediated in time, space, symbolic actions, and holy objects. They embraced Jesus' distinctive story as the basis for their calendar of remembering and celebrating. The crucifixion and resurrection of Jesus was and is the centerpoint of all Christian celebration and worship. The liturgy of the church focuses on this mystery. It is the central story we rehearse. It is the reality we are immersed in at our baptism. It is the mystery we receive in Holy Communion. Even the Free Church tradition, which has tended to minimize observance of the liturgical calendar, celebrates Easter.

In time the church added another cycle that focused on the incarnation of the eternal Word in Jesus. And so, Christians today keep time using two great cycles: the *cycle of life*, with Good Friday–Easter at its center, and the *cycle of light*, with Christmas–Epiphany at its center. Each cycle has a preparatory season: Lent leads to Holy Week and the fifty days of Easter, and Advent leads to twelve days of Christmas, which end on Epiphany, January 6.

Over time the early church incorporated the Gospel stories of Matthew, Mark, Luke, and John as the content of the calendar's cycles for celebration and remembrances. Rather than being a burden, the Christian calendar was and still is an imaginative evangelical tool for proclaiming Christ as Savior and Lord and for calling people to conversion. During the third and fourth centuries, the Jerusalem church was especially creative and evangelical in commemorating the events of Jesus' life, particularly during Holy Week. A journal from Egeria, a fourth-century Spanish pilgrim, and the mystagogical sermons (sermons about the meaning of baptism) of Cyril of Jerusalem reveal that worship was an intense and deeply moving experience at Golgotha, the Mount of Olives, and the tomb.[3] Even beyond Holy Week, the vigil of the resurrection was kept each Saturday from sunset to cockcrow.

In other words, our liturgical inheritance from the second to the sixth centuries is not organized around doctrine or philosophy but around God's victory in the story of Jesus and the people of Israel. The Jerusalem congregation processed from the various holy places with the singing of hymns; reenactments and prayer; lighting of candles; listening to narrations from the Gospels; and making use of oil, water, fasting, sacred space, and light. Egeria repeatedly notes the archdeacon's dismissal sending the people to their homes to eat and announcing the next time and place of gathering.

You can see a rhythm of gathering, observance and prayer, dismissal, departure, and return. The liturgy was a catechizing process; it was formational at deep levels. In her narration of Holy Week, Egeria notes again and again that the catechumens, those preparing to be baptized, are among the throng making pilgrimage. In his postbaptismal sermons, Cyril interprets what the newly baptized have experienced. So I use the word *evangelical* quite literally. Through liturgy the church "playfully" formed people in the gospel, the *evangelium*, both those already baptized and walking the path of discipleship and those preparing to be baptized.[4]

However, over time the church moved from immediacy of liturgical celebration to more distant observance. In *Worshipping Ecumenically,* Per Harling summarizes the history of Christian worship:

- "In the earlier Christian churches worship was something *done* in memory and in praise of the risen Christ." The focus was on *experience and full participation.* The whole assembly enacted worship and served God as a priestly people. Worship got into the people's neurons, muscles, and bones!

- "During the middle ages worship became something *said* in memory and in praise of the risen Christ." The focus was on *recitation and enactment* by the priest. Worship got into the people's eyes and ears, but their role as active celebrants was diminished.

- "During the Protestant Reformation worship became something *heard* (and understood) in memory and in praise of the risen Christ." Worship was *cerebration*—it got into the minds of the people.[5]

Note the reduced levels of engagement and participation. God's playground got shrunk! Thankfully, the last century of liturgical renewal and Pentecostalism have invited the "enlightenment" church to recover a sense of holy play that involves the full range of our worship capacity. Further, attention to multiple learning styles (multiple intelligences) has reinforced the urgency of this recovery of worship as holy play, welcoming all people to participate. Liturgical renewal is an attempt to recover "full, conscious, and active participation" of the assembly.[6]

The Deep Dynamics of the Calendar and Lectionary

The liturgical year is both a calendar and a lectionary—a schedule of seasons and special days with an accompanying table of Bible readings from three divisions of scripture: the Old Testament, the New Testament letters, and the four canonical Gospels. The story of the present-day three-year Sunday lectionaries is one that needs wider telling and greater appreciation.[7] It is a cause for rejoicing that Roman Catholics and many Protestant churches use essentially the same table of readings. This common ground invites greater dialogue and a sense of sharing around the table of the Word, even when we are not yet able to share around the table of the Eucharist.

The calendar and lectionary are interdependent. The calendar shapes and guides the selection of readings for the two great cycles around Easter and Christmas. The readings give narrative richness and content to the days and seasons of the Christian year. How local churches use the calendar and lectionary varies. Some churches work with the calendar independent of the lectionary, observing the seasons and festal days but choosing Bible readings on some other basis. Some use the lectionary as a pool of biblical texts for sermon passages but don't harness its power to focus Christian celebration of the mystery of God's creating and redeeming grace. Best practice suggests using the calendar and lectionary readings together. Congregations that employ both resources have a solid pathway for a lifelong and an ever-deepening spiral of proclamation, conversion, sacramental participation, and missional service.

By utilizing the calendar and lectionary, Christian liturgical prayer avoids preaching a set of rules to live by or a philosophy divorced from the action and mission of God. Calendar and lectionary ground us in the deeply narrative nature of the human psyche and of the biblical revelation.

We are inherently storied beings. Much of popular media, from magazines to films to video games, is driven by our hunger for finding ourselves in the story. By deep remembering and celebrative rehearsal of God's action in Christ, the church inhabits God's story and continuously refreshes its imagination. Vital liturgical worship continually "populates" our inner world. Indeed, worship is world making, creating and inviting us to participate in an alternative reality. It is as basic as learning to pray fully, consciously, and actively, "Your kingdom come, your will be done. . . . For the kingdom, the power, and the glory are yours now and for ever." Christian liturgy can and ought to be dangerous to the status quo when participants recognize that a struggle is going on—the values and vision of God's reign stand in stark contrast to those of the dominant culture. Most churches have yet to discover how transforming and dangerous the liturgy of Christ is! The liturgy still waits for us.

Most churches have yet to discover how transforming and dangerous the liturgy of Christ is! The liturgy still waits for us.

Without this continuous and ever-deepening rehearsal of God's story, the church develops amnesia. As resistance to seeing the world as defined by dominant or popular culture, the Judeo-Christian liturgical tradition practices grateful remembrance. The Greek word for this kind of remembrance is *anamnesis. Anamnesis* is the antidote for amnesia. The antidote for forgetting who we are is to gather for worship in which we remember, rehearse, and thank God for all that God has done in Christ from the start of creation until Christ's coming again. *Anamnesis* is done in the liturgy of Word and sacrament.

This liturgical community is not ultimately identified with or rooted in any current cultural context. In baptism we are made a part of the new creation in Christ. I sometimes ask people, "How big is the new creation? Is it bigger than your church? Bigger than the United States of America? Bigger than our solar system?" The liturgy that forms us transcends boundaries of time and space. It includes all Christians in every time and place. They accompany us in the liturgy and in daily life. The new creation includes all that we can see through our telescopes and more. We can hardly imagine the scope of what God is up to! Yet there is a distinctive shape to our engagement with the new creation.

Susan J. White describes the spirituality fostered by the liturgy as one in which we "learn to walk with the dead."[8] *Anamnesis*, enabled by the calendar, lectionary, and liturgical prayer, collapses the distance between "then" and "now" so that the redemptive acts of God are always present. In a sense the liturgy takes us through the wardrobe to the world where everything is at stake and the Lion is the martyred champion on the stone table. This is why White describes the church as "a community with permeable boundaries."[9] We commune with the saints living and dead. We are formed in a sense of being connected to God and all of creation. By the means of grace practiced in worship, we join with creation's praise of God from its genesis until its consummation. We dare to chime in "with angels and archangels, and with all the company of heaven" in ascribing holiness and glory to God.

Continuing with White's consideration of permeable boundaries, this formation of community has a deeply ethical dimension. Immersed and communed in the love of God, we relativize our boundaries—the boundaries between varieties of Christian belief and practice (Baptists, Presbyterians, and Catholics), the living and the dead (making communion of the saints and ancestors a living experience), and the local community and the world at large. So the liturgy bears fruit in us as we discover that we are to be the body of Christ for the world, and we are to relate to those marginalized by poverty and racism in a Christlike manner. Here we come to the eschatological punch of the liturgy: it is about ultimate survival rather than about our immediate success or well-being. That is exactly why our life and worship together center on a not-to-be-romanticized "old rugged cross."

This is precisely where much of the debate in the church occurs today. Is worship supposed to tilt toward commodification of the gospel, being geared to immediate relevance and application? Or will worship and witness lean toward what has ultimate power to fire the imagination and will to "seek the Lord while [God] may be found" (Isa. 55:6)? We must beware of worship that must be trendy, constantly reinvented, and never the same, always tickling our fancy! Such edgy worship may simply be rooted in the current culture, not in the deep dynamic of the gospel that calls us from the "tumult of our life's wild, restless sea."

> Jesus calls us o'er the tumult
> of our life's wild, restless sea;
> day by day his sweet voice soundeth,
> saying, "Christian, follow me."[10]

In the liturgy Christ is not past; he becomes our contemporary. *We* are delivered, healed, restored to sight. *We* are forgiven, find our true voices, and are freed for joyful service. *We* experience Christ eating with us sinners. The opening of the liturgy expresses this anticipation and proclamation of the presence of Christ:

> The grace of the Lord Jesus Christ be with you.
> And also with you.
> The risen Christ is with us.
> Praise the Lord![11]

A Brief History of the Liturgical Year

Earlier in this chapter we reviewed the history of how Christians began to keep time with Christ. Now I invite you to consider a more detailed look at specific festivals and seasons of the Christian year.

Easter and Pentecost

In recent years a trend called the "emerging church" has surfaced in Christianity. This phenomenon recognizes and embraces the unfinished work of God in the church. In England, Australia, the United States, and other places in the world, young people are radically rethinking the nature of church, not so much in terms of institution as in practices that connect the ancient past and the present-future. Sometimes the emerging church is called "liquid church" because each local community seeks to be authentic and missional in its place. These communities boldly pay attention to where the risen Christ is going ahead of them in the present while they use the riches of the historic tradition as a compass.

This phenomenon is not new. At times in church history the tendency has been to act as though the church and its faith are set for all time. The emerging church is the antithesis of this mentality. It is not a denomination or institution so much

The Liturgical Year

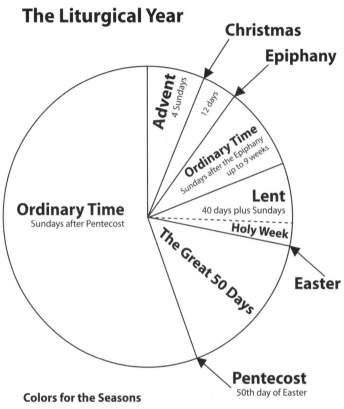

Advent
4 Sundays

Christmas

Epiphany

12 days

Ordinary Time
Sundays after the Epiphany
up to 9 weeks

Lent
40 days plus Sundays

Holy Week

Ordinary Time
Sundays after Pentecost

The Great 50 Days

Easter

Pentecost
50th day of Easter

Colors for the Seasons

Advent: Purple
Christmas through the Epiphany: White
Ordinary Time: Green
Lent: Purple
Holy Week: Scarlet
Easter/The Great 50 Days: White
Pentecost: Red

Note: The colors listed here are traditional. During Advent, some churches use blue, a color associated with hope. During Lent, some churches extend the use of purple through Holy Week rather than change to scarlet.

as faith communities living out their conviction that the church and its faith must always be "contextual." What God wants the church to be and look like in any culture and time in history is always emerging. Sometimes that means the church must make significant shifts in its ways of worship and in its understanding of how it is to address the surrounding culture. More often it means that the church has to reinterpret its inheritance (the scriptures, its central doctrines, its ministry, its ways of being community) for an emerging context.

Think of the liturgical calendar in this same vein. It emerged. One of the emergent practices in the early church was the date for celebrating Jesus' resurrection. Easter—the day of the Lord's resurrection, the day of the new creation, the eighth day—was the defining fact of all time for the first Christians, but the date of Easter varied. Some areas celebrated the Resurrection on the Sunday after Passover, and some (Asia Minor) celebrated Easter on the Jewish Passover itself, primarily as a commemoration of the death of Jesus. In either case, Easter was closely tied to Passover. Eventually the Sunday celebration emerged as the dominant practice.

Christian worship and Christian existence hinge on the resurrection of Jesus Christ. The imagery and language used by Christians, particularly in liturgical worship, is rich and multi-layered. Hymns, readings, and prayers celebrate and make connections between the story of Christ's passion, death, and resurrection and Israel's slavery, bondage, and exodus through the waters of the Red Sea. Indeed, the story of God's deliverance of Israel is archetypal for God's "play" with us in the liturgy. Easter, and particularly the service of Easter Vigil, is our rehearsal of passage from death to life, from slavery to freedom, from darkness to light. On the night of the vigil we sing an Easter proclamation called the Exsultet. This extended praise recounts the mighty acts of God in Israel's exodus with strong connections to the work of Christ in his death and resurrection. The effect is to proclaim that Easter is our Passover and exodus from slavery to sin and death.[12]

The Easter Vigil is kept sometime after sunset on the Saturday before Easter. Some churches start as soon as darkness falls, some at or near midnight, and some before dawn on Sunday. If you have not experienced an Easter Vigil, I encourage you to find a church known for strong liturgical worship and to participate in its vigil.

Let's return to our story of how Easter evolved in liturgical observance. By the third century Easter emerged as a unitive rite called the Triduum. This three-day observance of the passion, death, burial, and resurrection of Jesus Christ began at sunset on Thursday and continued through sunset on Easter Day. It was an extended rehearsal of the transition from death to life. While many churches today observe separate days— Holy Thursday evening, Good Friday, Holy Saturday, and Easter—the more ancient practice is to view them as one rite. Remember the rhythm of gathering, observance and prayer, dismissal, departure, and return that Egeria records in her diary.

The Triduum (meaning "three days") includes the Easter Vigil, the primal liturgical service for Christians. The service consists of four parts: the service of light, the service of the Word, the service of water, and the service of the Meal. The service of light involves kindling a bonfire outdoors and lighting the Paschal candle that burns at all services from Easter to Pentecost and at baptisms and funerals throughout the year. (See illus. of candle on the next page.) The Paschal candle symbolizes both the pillar of fire that went before Israel (Exod. 13:21-22) and Christ, our light and illumination. The service of the Word includes ample readings from the Bible that tell the

Paschal Candle

story of creation, covenant, and exodus. Like the Ents, the giant treelike characters in Tolkien's *The Lord of the Rings*, we take a long time to rehearse and delight in telling our story. In the service of water, the church baptizes candidates and reaffirms its baptismal covenant. Then all, the newly baptized and the faithful, celebrate the Eucharist in the service of the table.

The observation of Pentecost, the fiftieth day after Easter, began as early as the second century. The fifty days between Easter and Pentecost served as a period of rejoicing in the grace of the risen Christ and exploring the life of the church as an Easter people. By the fourth century the Day of Pentecost had become a celebration of the gift of the Holy Spirit.

CHRISTMAS, EPIPHANY, AND LENT

We observe Christmas on December 25, and many modern Christians believe Christmas to be as ancient as any Christian celebration. However, until the fourth century no firm evidence exists to support the celebration of Christmas or Epiphany. Indeed, the date of the celebration varied. Churches in Rome and North Africa celebrated Jesus' birth on December 25. Other churches observed the Nativity on January 6.

Why did some Christians set the date as December 25? One hypothesis is that they computed the date of Jesus' conception as occurring on the same date as his death, calculated by some to be March 25. According to this imaginative yet literalist thinking, he would have been born nine months later. Another hypothesis, based on "counterattraction," proposes that Christians countered the pagan feast of the "birth of the invincible Sun" at the winter solstice with a celebration of Jesus' birth as the Sun of Righteousness (Mal. 4:2) who brings light and life in the shortened days of winter. Note that our liturgical celebrations are oriented to the experience of the Northern Hemisphere, and the seasonal aspects do not align with the experience of Christians in the Southern Hemisphere. The emerging global awareness of the church has yet to deal with the Northern Hemisphere's privilege in regard to the Christian liturgical calendar.

The important issue here is not the historicity of the date of Jesus' birth, for Christmas is far more than a sentimental nativity feast and a historical event. Despite all that our imaginations, inspired by the Lukan and Matthean birth narratives, bring to this festival, for the ancient emerging church, Christmas was the Feast of the Incarnation. It had a strong doctrinal and apologetic purpose over against those who insisted that Jesus was adopted as God's Son at baptism. The prologue to John's Gospel (John 1:1-18) and the readings for Christmas Day in the *Revised Common Lectionary* punctuate this strong attentiveness to the eternal Word that became incarnate in Jesus Christ. The celebration of the twelve days of Christmas, concluding on Epiphany (January 6), interweaves the narrative with this high doctrine of who Jesus was and is so that we encounter him not simply as an innocent and beautiful infant but as the divine and eternal Word, the second person of the Trinity.

What about Epiphany (January 6)? The celebration of Epiphany continues God's play in and with the church. In Asia Minor the computation of the date of Jesus' death occurring on the same day as his conception applied. In the East the church simply reckoned the date on a different calendar. As with the varying dates of observing Jesus' birth, the focus of the celebration was not the same in all places. The focus varied from highlighting the visit of Magi and the Nativity, to the baptism of Jesus, to his first miracle—the turning of water into wine at Cana.

Scholar Thomas J. Talley suggests that the reason for the diversity could be attributed to the pattern of the lectionary cycle.[13] The two principal modern lectionaries, the *Revised Common Lectionary* and the Roman Catholic *Lectionary for Sunday Mass*, share a characteristic with the lectionary of the Eastern Church at the time these celebrations were established. These lectionaries rotate the reading of the synoptic Gospels over a three-year period for a given Sunday. Thus, in one year Matthew tells the story of the Magi; in the next year Mark narrates the baptism of Jesus; and in the third year Luke tells of the Nativity. And John's Gospel, woven into the lectionary, begins Jesus' ministry with the wedding miracle at Cana.

Another scholar, Paul Bradshaw, speculates that pagan festivals called *epiphaneia* might have caused Christians to celebrate a counterattraction, or to assert that Christ was the fulfillment of truths dimly perceived in other religions.[14]

I hope you can see and appreciate two aspects of these emergent celebrations and practices: (1) they reflect a certain messiness that goes with the church's struggle to come to terms with Christ and who he is, and (2) worship is contextual—it developed in and sought to be faithful to its context in complex and dynamic cultural realities. Such awareness and appreciation allows us to recognize that God still plays with us as we seek to be faithful to our inheritance from the saints and to the contexts in which we live today.

In time all churches in the West observed both days, with the first emerging as celebration of the Nativity (December 25) and the second (January 6) continuing to carry diverse meanings. For the West, Epiphany focused on the visit of the Magi, while in the East it emphasized the baptism of Jesus or his first miracle at Cana. Attempting to include the varied strands of celebration, the *Revised Common Lectionary* follows this scheme of storytelling:

(A, B, and C are the three years of rotation. Where ABC occur together, it means that the same reading is used for all three years.)

Christmas Eve: Luke 2:1-20 (ABC)—Nativity

Christmas Day: John 1:1-14 (ABC)—Incarnation

Epiphany: Matthew 2:1-12 (ABC)—Magi

Baptism of the Lord (First Sunday after the Epiphany):

>   Matthew 3:13-17 (Year A)

>   Mark 1:4-11 (Year B)

>   Luke 3:15-17, 21-22 (Year C)

(Each of these readings focuses on Jesus' baptism.)

Second Sunday after the Epiphany:

>   John 1:29-42 (Year A)—John the Baptist: "Here is the Lamb of God . . ." and prospective disciples saying, "We have found the Messiah"

>   John 1:43-51 (Year B)—Nathaniel: "Rabbi, you are the Son of God!"

>   John 2:1-11 (Year C)—Cana: "Jesus did this, the first of his signs [changing water to wine] . . . and revealed his glory"

This detail illustrates how the church conserves what emerged over time by embracing and recasting it for use in its current context. Rather than one-for-one equivalence, the liturgy allows for inclusion of varied facets in its celebration of the gospel.

Interestingly, Lent also illustrates this emergence. We associate the six-week period called Lent with the Easter cycle, but it began as a period of fasting immediately after January 6 in the Egyptian Church. There Lent served as a period of preparation for those awaiting baptism and for penitents before they were allowed to return to the celebration of the Eucharist. Perhaps this was done to imitate the forty-day fast of Jesus following his baptism (Mark 1:9-13). In the fourth century many parts of the church adopted a forty-day fast, leading to baptism at the Easter Vigil.

EXPERIENCING THE CYCLES AND DAYS OF THE CALENDAR

While this history is interesting and important for scholarship, the valuable insights and formative potency of the church year can only be realized in experiencing the liturgy of the seasons in its richness and full array. Think of times when you found yourself transported in quiet wonder on the fourth Sunday of Advent, on Holy Thursday, or on Easter. Maybe it happened at a midnight Christmas Eve service as you sang, "Yea, Lord, we greet thee, born this happy morning." Or you recall kneeling at the chancel rail on Ash Wednesday as ashes were smudged on your forehead and you heard the words, "Remember that you are dust, and to dust you shall return" or "Repent, and believe the gospel." Or maybe you remember a time of foot washing after the reading of John 13 when you stepped forward and a child washed your feet, or you washed the pastor's feet. These are moments of encounter, of truth telling, and of abounding grace. They are singular moments, never to be repeated in quite the same way, and yet by them God's Spirit indwells us, shapes our affections, reorients our emotions, and we can say, "I am who I am because we were together in the room when the crucified and risen One stood among us and said, 'Peace be with you.'"

The liturgy of the Christian year is the communal setting where we are blessed with a shared memory. As we stand face-to-face and body to body with other members of the body of Christ, our imaginations are charged by fire, water, bread, wine, ashes, foot basins and towels, oil, and holy touch.

QUESTIONS FOR REFLECTION

1. As you reflect on your lived experience in the round of the Christian year, what moments in the liturgy stand out? How have such moments shaped and anchored you? Recalling one such moment, what was going on in the rest of your life that connected with those liturgical moments?

2. How does Psalm 77 illuminate the discussion of amnesia and *anamnesis* (p. 67)? Who is charged with not remembering? How does active recollection of God's past action reshape the psalmist's current outlook?

3. How does recognizing the messiness of the emergence of the liturgical calendar help you appreciate the cycles and seasons of worship we follow today?

CHAPTER 4

By Water and the Spirit:
Living Out Our Baptism

The modern approach to education is to understand by analysis, dissection, and review of literature. The ancient and emerging postmodern way of pedagogy is to experience something, then to reflect on the experience.

I invite you to experience baptism in a fresh way by means of a story. As you read, you may encounter several terms or practices new to you. True to the method of experience preceding reflection and analysis, simply enjoy the story, even what is strange to your internal dictionary. Remember, liturgy is God's playground.

EASTER IN EPHESUS: A THIRD-CENTURY TALE

As they had done during the months of scrutiny and instruction in the way of Christians, Lydia's grandparents stood with her now in the crowded room. Small oil lamps burned, giving only enough light to illumine the faces of the presbyters, deacons, and her fellow candidates for baptism, who also were accompanied by their sponsors. On the way to the church they had passed the smoldering remains of a bonfire.

Lydia stood shivering on the cold stone floor in the pre-dawn, wondering what would happen next. Whatever it was, she wanted it to happen quickly. Lydia was a fourteen-year-old Ephesian, but she was eager to become a citizen of heaven. She knew she was ready to be one of them, as she had told her grandparents some weeks before.

Without speaking, a deacon motioned the women to one side of the gathering, and the men to the other. A phalanx of male and female deacons formed a barrier between the two groups. Lydia could hear singing nearby but couldn't distinguish the words. Suddenly there was a loud banging on the door. The porter quickly opened it, and the bishop entered as all became still. The wizened man walked with a limp that some said he got as a result of being tortured in the persecution forty years before. Turning his gaze toward the candidates, he barked, "Take off your clothes." No one protested! This was the moment of leaving behind everything—even their clothes—to be newborn daughters and sons of God.

A presbyter directed the candidates to spit repudiation on the devil and renounce all the works of darkness. "Now turn east," the presbyter directed, and they saw dawn's first light glowing golden through the alabaster windows. The rising sun was nature's witness to the rising of Jesus Christ from the dead. Like the virgins in the Gospel story, Lydia and the others were awaiting their moment to welcome the Bridegroom in baptism. As a deacon named Dora anointed Lydia's body with oil, she welcomed the cleansing rub of protection, both from the night's cold air and from the possibility that she might turn back from the Way, as her parents had done a few years before. *Will I be able to remain faithful?* she wondered.

Presently they moved through a doorway into another room with a pool in the center. The baptistery walls and ceiling were alive with stories, images of water and oil and the Spirit: Jonah, cast overboard, and a fish, jaws wide open, waiting to swallow him; Moses with his rod extended over the sea, as walls of water closed on Pharaoh's soldiers and chariots, and the people of Israel huddled safely on dry ground; a man bathing in the Jordan, one leg, white with leprosy, still on the bank, and the other, pink and new like baby's skin, in the water. On the ceiling John the Baptist stood on the bank of the Jordan, pouring water on Jesus, who was standing in the river. To one side demons scurried away, and above Jesus a hand reached down from heaven, as a dove descended toward Jesus' head. The scene was a mirror image of what was about to happen, though Lydia and the other catechumens didn't know it.

Without a word, Justina, another deacon, led Lydia down the steps into the pool. Above, on the edge of the pool, the bishop bent over, tapped Lydia on the shoulder with his staff, and asked her, "Do you believe in God the Father, the Maker of heaven and earth?" She hesitated, unsure of whether to answer aloud or just think her response. Justina squeezed her arm and pointed to the bishop, prompting her to answer aloud. "Yes, I do," said Lydia. And before she knew what was happening, Justina, a stout woman, pushed her under the water. Lydia struggled back up, gasping for the breath she had not taken after her answer. She wanted to cry but didn't know why. Then the bishop asked, "Lydia, do you believe in Jesus Christ, God's only Son; born of the Virgin Mary; suffered under Pontius Pilate; was crucified, died, and buried; and descended to the dead? Do you believe that he was raised on the third day and ascended into heaven?" This time Lydia did not pause but shot back, "I do," grabbing her nose as Justina again pushed her under the waves like Jonah being cast overboard. A third time the bishop tapped her on the shoulder with his staff and asked, "Lydia, do you believe in the Holy Spirit, the holy catholic church, the forgiveness of sins, the resurrection of the body, and the life everlasting?" This time it was beginning to be fun as she found the rhythm of call, response, and dunk! Justina guided Lydia up the steps to her grandparents, Marcus and Julia, who were waiting to embrace her with a towel and words of rejoicing. Then they clothed her in a simple white garment.

One by one the other candidates were immersed as Lydia stood in the warm glow of lamps on the wall sconces, and sunlight began to peek in through the clerestory windows at the top of the room.

Vigilant for what would happen next in this drama of passing from death to life, Lydia saw a presbyter named John approaching her and the others now dressed in white. The fragrance preceded him—a sweet, bitter smell of olive oil mixed with myrrh. He poured the oil over her head and lavishly rubbed it on her face, shoulders, hands, and feet as the bishop prayed, "Blessed God who sent the Holy Spirit upon your child Jesus at the Jordan, anoint with holiness and the Spirit these your servants. Ever defend and protect them from the deceit of the devil, inspiring them with your grace to be always true to the way of Jesus . . ." His voice trailed off as Lydia recalled her grandmother's tears for her parents, who had turned from Christ under the pressure of the emperor's threats.

Her attention snapped back to the present moment as she heard the sound of singing on the other side of the double doors. The words were no longer indistinct: *"Christos aneste . . ."* ("Christ is risen . . ."). The singing grew louder and louder as if faith was growing with excitement. The bishop interrupted the singing as he pounded on the doors with his fist and chanted in a different key, *"Christos aneste!"* Lydia heard the people inside join the chant, singing:

Christ is risen from the dead
trampling down death by death
and on those in the tombs, bestowing life!

The bishop, standing at the now open doors, called out, "Let the newborn of God join the assembly." There in the crowded assembly room were the faces of those Lydia had seen on Sundays when she had gathered to hear the reading of the holy scriptures and the preaching of the bishop. They looked like angels rejoicing. Heaven was opened in proud welcome as the bishop led the newly born into the midst of the assembly.

"Now, dear children of God, born this night as Christians into the catholic church, you will feast with us on the precious body and blood of Christ. But first, you must drink the gustatory drink of the Promised Land." Immediately and just once, Justina put a cup to Lydia's lips, and she sipped the warm, nourishing sweetness of milk laced with honey. The taste would linger in her memory for a lifetime.

Then the assembly divided left and right to reveal a table behind which the bishop now stood. There she saw bread and a large cup. Looking deeply into the people's eyes, he extended his hands and said, "The Lord be with you," to which they responded, "And also with you." Then when he said, "Lift up your hearts," Lydia felt she had come home to a people who were her people. She squeezed the hands of her grandparents on each side of her; they were now, more importantly, her brother and sister in the faith, along with all the others who this night would share the bread and cup of salvation in Love's service for all the days to come.

By Water and the Spirit: Living Out Our Baptism 85

Lydia left the assembly rejoicing, her heart bursting with song. Words were inadequate to express her feelings. She was still a citizen of Ephesus, but more importantly, she belonged to a chosen race, a royal priesthood, God's own people. She could only imagine where that would lead her as she stepped into the warm sunlight of the new day.

Baptism with Something at Stake

Perhaps you have never experienced a baptism done with such power, such lavishness of symbolic action, and such embodied communal celebration. That is why I tell the story—as a kind of remedial and imaginative apprehension of what we have missed in most present-day baptismal services and as an invitation to greater fullness of ritual action and participation. Notice the rich array of leadership roles in the ritual, both presiding and assisting: a porter, male and female deacons, the bishop as presider, the presbyters, and sponsors. Note also the very active engagement of the assembly. The members were much more than observers. Imagine how we today might be formed more deeply in faith and imagination by such an experience. How might our baptismal celebrations become such memorable sensory events? more embedded in a community formed over time?

Our more recent baptismal and eucharistic practice has suffered from a minimalism that asks, "What is the least (water, fuss, involvement, trouble, time) we must do to *validly* baptize people and welcome them into the faith community?" North Americans tend to be efficiency oriented, even in the church and particularly when we don't recognize what is at stake. So we seek to use as little water as possible and to "get it done" with as little fuss and fanfare as possible. We squeeze baptism into a worship service that must not exceed an hour.

So efficiency plays into the question of validity. Neither efficiency nor validity is the issue in Lydia's story. Instead, enactment of God's amazing and robust grace is the issue. Baptism, sacramentally understood, is Christ's act in the church. The sacraments are primarily actions supported by words, not primarily words. And the action is primarily God's.

As we see in the story, baptism is washing in the triune name of God, laying on of hands and anointing with oil and the Holy Spirit, and nourishing and feeding the newly born. It is God's gracious initiative embracing Lydia and each of us, incorporating us into the body of Christ; joining us to all that God has done and is doing in Christ Jesus by the Holy Spirit. Yes, our human response is required, as in Lydia's answering the questions of faith and the community's active celebration and faithful living of the gospel in their daily lives. But chiefly, baptism is an "outward and visible sign of an inward and spiritual grace" enacted in the rite of initiation.[1]

Baptism is an unrepeatable event because *God* includes us in the one covenant made by the baptism of Christ in his dying and rising. It is not merely an individual covenant between each person and God, though each of us needs to personally respond to the grace God extends to us in the sacrament.[2] Rather, baptism is our entering into the covenant community that God has embraced in Christ's passion, death, and resurrection. It is our corporate entrance into the Paschal mystery of union with Christ and his church. When and where the church enacts the sacraments powerfully, deeply, and confidently, it acknowledges, confesses, and embodies God's action. This does not mean that baptism is null and void if celebrated in minimalist ways. It does mean that how we celebrate the sacraments matters if we are to enact what we profess God is doing.

The United Methodist ritual puts it this way:

> Through the Sacrament of Baptism
> *we are* initiated into Christ's holy church.
> We are incorporated into God's mighty acts of salvation
> and *given new birth* through water and the Spirit.
> All this is God's gift, offered to us without price.
> (emphasis added)[3]

Notice the receptive tone of the language: "We are . . . initiated . . . incorporated . . . given new birth." In baptism we receive God's grace.

The Presbyterian ritual text introduces the sacrament in a slightly more expansive way:

> Obeying the word of our Lord Jesus,
> and confident of his promises,
> we baptize those whom God has called.
>
> In baptism *God claims us,*
> and *seals us to show that we belong to God.*
> God *frees us* from sin and death,
> *uniting us* with Jesus Christ in his death and resurrection.
> By water and the Holy Spirit,
> *we are made members of the church, the body of Christ,*
> and *joined to Christ's ministry of love, peace, and justice.*
> (emphasis added)[4]

Note the significance of baptism proclaimed in these two introductory statements.

- *Trust in Christ's promises:* The ritual action expresses the church's faith and trust that God has birthed and sustains us in the body of Christ.

- *God's initiative:* Understood as sacrament, the rite is not chiefly the action of the church but the gracious action of God on behalf of "those whom God has called" in order to "claim" and "seal" them, giving them "new birth" in union with "Christ's ministry of love, peace, and justice." Baptism signifies the incredibly generous and cosmic work of God for the sake of bringing peace and justice to the whole creation.

- *New birth:* We are born into a new reality; we are "born from above," to use the imagery of Jesus in his night dialogue with Nicodemus (John 3:1-10). In baptism we are born anew to live in God's new creation, and the liturgy again and again immerses us in this alternative to the economic and political powers we encounter daily.

- *United with Christ in his death and resurrection:* Union with Christ is a primary motif in Christian reflection on the baptismal covenant and is supported by the classic words of Paul in Romans 6:1-11. This is the Paschal mystery: in baptism we die with Christ that we may also share a resurrection like his. This rite becomes a paradigm for the rest of our life in which we shall again and again experience dyings and risings with Christ, including our physical dying in the hope of resurrection. We are given an increasing fearlessness to risk and face danger and death for the sake of Christ and his coming reign of peace and justice.

- *Organic union with the church:* Much of the modern church has demonstrated an institutional understanding of church membership. We "join" the church as a conscious and deliberate act and become members in the sense of being dues-paying and responsible participants. But now many churches are recovering the more ancient and biblical "organic" understanding of membership. We are members in the metaphoric sense that Paul so imaginatively describes in 1 Corinthians 12: we are members of the "body of Christ" just as the hands, eyes, ears, feet, brain, and heart are members of the physical body. We are members one of another, interdependent on one another for our life together as the community witnessing to the coming reign of God. This concept is fundamental to our understanding of the church. Theologians call it *ecclesiology* (compound of "called" and "out" in Greek). The church is the *ecclesia*—the assembly of those called out for God's special service. In liturgy and life we are continuously being born and formed as the living embodiment of Christ in the world.

- *Identification with Christ's ministry:* We are "joined to Christ's ministry." This is the corollary of being the body of Christ understood in a dynamic sense. Our identity is missional. We are a city on a hill, light for the entire world to see, salt penetrating present reality with the flavor and preserving power of Christ's love and justice.

This list by no means exhausts the images and meanings to be experienced and explored in our baptism. What other images and meanings do you recognize that could be added to this list? Washing? Regeneration? Illumination? Exodus? Anointing? Massaging? Embracing? In baptism we participate not only in a ritual moment; we are immersed in the depth of the love and life of the triune God. We can never exhaust the connections between what God begins and continues in all of our life experiences.

Many churches now invite the gathered community to "remember your baptism and be thankful."[5] The invitation is not to remember the actual moment of baptism, though that may be part of our response. Rather, the invitation is to rejoice in and recall the life and identity we have been given in the body of Christ. It is an invitation to take the fact of our baptism off the shelf, dust it off, and renew the sacred covenant in which we have been joined with Jesus and his whole church.

For example, I was baptized as a youth in 1957. I went through a preparatory class with the pastor, but I had little idea of what baptism was all about. From a human perspective, I was DOA instead of newly born. But God's grace was up to more than I could know or understand. I was born anew to a life of grace that was yet to unfold.

In 1962 as a college freshman, I found myself immersed in an evangelical environment and in relationships that probed and provoked me to come out of the fog of my inchoate adolescent faith. One morning in worship, the pastor's sermon seemed to be addressed to me. I felt a distinct prompting to respond to the invitation to discipleship. But I resisted what I sensed to be a call for giving myself to God in trust and unreserved service. I sang all of the hymn stanzas, each time thinking I would step forward on the next one. I didn't. I did, however, admit to this inner struggle to a friend on the way back to the campus. The conversation did not relieve the call I felt to give myself to God; it only intensified the "crisis." In that pressure-cooker moment, I prayed tearfully: "God, if you want me, I am yours. I will go where you want me to go and say what you want me to say." At that moment I gave as much of myself as I could to God, with no strings attached.

Serendipitously—and I realized this later—it was five years to the day after my baptism that I experienced this deep, inner dying and rising with Christ. What God had begun in baptism took a giant step forward as the Spirit moved me more deeply into the Paschal mystery. Of course, I did not know or use the phrase "Paschal mystery" then. I simply knew that something powerful was shaking my foundations like a tsunami, like a mighty wind, like an undeniable vocation. Christ's act in the church came home to roost in the very details and direction of my life. Baptism anticipates a lifetime of such formative moments. Baptism is always more than a religious moment in the church building. It is an immersion into the life of grace that buoys us up into eternal life.

As you reflect on your life's journey, what connections do you see between your experience of the life of grace and the marking of your life as one of the baptized? Before moving on with this book, stop to be aware of what comes to the surface of your attention. Take a few minutes to rest in reflective thought.

BASIC UNDERSTANDINGS

Baptism touches a number of themes and dimensions of our life in Christ.

1. *As a ritual act with roots in the scriptures, it evokes a rich array of images, symbols, and meanings.* Baptism marks us as disciples (Matt. 28:19). We receive the forgiveness of sins and the gift of the Holy Spirit indwelling our lives (Acts 2:38), and we are adopted as the sons and daughters of God (Mark 1:1-4; Gal. 4:4-7). We are born from above, born anew (John 3:5-7). We experience death and resurrection with Christ (Rom. 6:3-11), the washing away of sin (1 Cor. 6:11), and sealing as guarantee (2 Cor. 1:21-22). We are washed, justified, sanctified (2 Cor. 6:9-11), and participate in Israel's exodus from captivity as those saved through the flood (1 Cor. 10:1-2; 1 Pet. 3:20-21). We are clothed with new garments (Gal. 3:27) and joined in a new humanity

without distinctions as to background, gender, race, or status (Gal. 3:28). We receive illumination (Eph. 5:14) and renewal by the Spirit (Titus 3:5).

2. *Baptism is both God's initiating grace in the world and our human and communal response to that grace in faith and service.* This is another way of recognizing our diversity around baptism. Most Christian denominations understand baptism as a *sacrament* (what God does), incorporating us into the church and into Christ and giving us new birth by water and the Spirit. Some denominations, such as Baptists, understand the act primarily as an *ordinance* (what we do) as a response of obedience, renouncing evil and sin and professing faith in Christ in union with the church. Denominations that hold a sacramental view of baptism also explicitly or tacitly understand that there must be a response to what God does.

3. *Baptism signifies Christ's action in the church.* We participate, act in faith, and believe, but it is Christ's action by the Spirit that is primary. Baptism is an action of the believing community, in the name of the triune God, using water by sprinkling, pouring, or immersion.

4. *Baptism is both an event and a process of formation* whereby we are initiated into life in Christ and into his body, the church. It is part of a lifelong process. At its best, spiritual formation immerses us into the faithful community before and after our baptism. Relationships form; we hold one another accountable for the life of faith, hope, and love into which we have been baptized. The presence of the font at the entrance or some other visible place in the worship space reminds us of this shared grace and accountability.

We can point to it and say, "There is our bathtub! This is our fountain of life."

5. *Baptism is an unrepeatable event.* Because it is God's action, baptism is a sure sign of God's inexhaustible love and grace. In response to this gift of union with Christ, we may at times be unfaithful, but even our unfaithfulness does not break God's covenant with us. Christ continues to make the grace of relationship available to us. Another way of saying it is that we can't get into a room we are already in! Our living may not always reflect our commitment to the baptismal covenant, but God's claim and mark upon us is indelible and lifelong. Most ecumenical churches do not "rebaptize" persons, for such an action impugns the faithfulness of God and wounds the body of Christ.

When we are periodically called to remember our baptism and be thankful, we are invited to remember who and whose we are for this part of our journey: this day, this week, this daily life in the web of relationships that make up our home, leisure, work, local, church, and global communities.

FORMATIVE DIMENSIONS OF OUR COMMUNAL EXPERIENCE OF BAPTISM

The action of the gathered community is ritual play that shapes us. The liturgical renewal movement, implemented in the last thirty years, has recovered a much richer and deeper sense of the communal celebration of the baptismal covenant. Liturgy, however personal and inward some of its moments may be, always involves the action of the faithful assembly. As chapter 2 noted, even daily prayer prayed alone is still a participation in the ongoing prayer of the whole church.

Baptism is done in the presence of the gathered church, hopefully with members of other churches present, to signify that a new person is being welcomed and incorporated into the body of Christ. Indeed, the faith professed at your baptism was not your personal faith, even if you were a youth or an adult and were able to declare your belief. Rather, you joined in the communal profession of the universal church, the "holy catholic church" as we say in the creeds. You professed the faith of the church, not simply your personal credo. In baptism you shared a communal experience of water and the Spirit. "This is our bathtub! This is our fountain of life." We live out of what God gave us for the rest of our lives. As someone put it, we "live wet." We live like fish in a new water-world in relationship to the great fish, Jesus Christ, the Son of God.[6] In a preface to the Great Thanksgiving in the Book of Common Prayer (p. 378), the priest prays: "For by water and the Holy Spirit you have made us a new people in Jesus Christ our Lord, to show forth your glory in all the world." This is lifelong communal venture.

In baptism we are made part of God's new creation, the anticipatory community actively waiting for all things to be made new. Congregations that live in the new creation now and actively wait for its fulfillment are spiritually alive. The tragedy of spiritually dying congregations is that, though they formally became communities of the eighth day through baptism, they lack the hearts and eyes to perceive the new things God is doing. When pastors and congregations perpetuate the sense of baptism as a private transaction between God and the baptized person, as if baptism gave each individual a ticket to eternal life, they misshape the consciousness of the church and compromise the vision of discipleship. In baptism we become a mutually accountable community, watching over one another in love.

How well do you and your congregation live attentively to the Spirit in your relationships and situations? Do your congregational prayers and preaching give witness to the places where God is doing a new thing in the midst of pain and the struggle for peace and justice? In what ways do you connect the renunciation and profession in the rite of baptism with living a disciplined spirituality in relationship to other members of the body of Christ?

- *Baptism is grounded in the Paschal mystery.* While the sacrament can be celebrated anytime the congregation gathers, the calendar and lectionary hinge on Easter and other days centered on Christ our Passover as days for baptism (Baptism of the Lord, All Saints' Day, Pentecost, Trinity Sunday). On the Palm Sunday after that March day of conversion I mentioned earlier, I remember reading Paul's electric confession: "I have been crucified with Christ; and it is no longer I who live, but it is Christ who lives in me. And the life I now live in the flesh I live by faith in the Son of God, who loved me and gave himself for me" (Gal. 2:19-20). That, in a nutshell, is the Paschal mystery: life in union with Christ in his dying and rising. Some call it Christ mysticism.

  Rather than conforming to a set of religious rules and ethical guidelines for the moral life, liturgy forms us in a Paschal spirituality. We live because Christ lives in us. In baptism we died a death like his. In baptism we rise to share in Christ's death-defying love, even when it means sacrifice and loss for us in the short term. In the weekly liturgy we again and again meet the risen Lord around font, Bible, and table, welcoming his life into our lives and proclaiming, "Christ has died; Christ is risen; Christ will come again."

The recovery of the practice of Easter Vigil from the ancient church (described in Lydia's story at the first of this chapter) is a gift to the contemporary church.[7] The vigil situates the church's life at the epicenter of God's new creation. In the rich use of fire and light, story and song, water and oil, and holy food and drink as the vessels and vehicles of remembering who we are, we reconnect with Christ, whom we serve. One of the distinguishing songs of the Easter Vigil is an ancient proclamation to God and all creation called the Exsultet. Observe how this Paschal chant makes use of two central narratives: the Passover/Exodus story and the drama of Christ's crucifixion and resurrection:

> It is truly right and good, always and everywhere, with our whole heart and mind and voice, to praise you, the invisible, almighty, and eternal God, and your only-begotten Son, Jesus Christ our Lord; for *he is the true Paschal Lamb*, who at the feast of the Passover paid for us the debt of Adam's sin, and by his blood delivered your faithful people.
>
> *This is the night*, when you brought our [ancestors], the children of Israel, out of bondage in Egypt, and led them through the Red Sea on dry land.
>
> *This is the night, when all who believe in Christ are delivered* from the gloom of sin, and are restored to grace and holiness of life.
>
> *This is the night*, when Christ broke the bonds of death and hell, and rose victorious from the grave. (emphasis added)[8]

Some versions of the Easter Proclamation (Exsultet) are even more explicit in saying, "This is our Passover feast."

Even if your congregation does not celebrate the Easter Vigil, I encourage you to visit a congregation that does and to experience the fullness of this "night truly blessed." Your experience of it may awaken you more deeply to the Paschal mystery. Who knows? You may invite others to go with you and together decide to urge your congregation to include Easter Vigil in its liturgical calendar and practice.

- *Baptism is both an event and a communal journey.* This understanding is crucial for the church as a faith-forming and disciple-making community. It is critical to our recovering an evangelical and universal way of making disciples of those God calls to the waters and the Spirit. Baptism is not an isolated event; it is embedded in the very way the church lives its life together, and in how it welcomes and forms new Christians. We are in the early years of a contemporary recovery of the ancient church's way of initiating persons. The journey's name in the ancient church was the *catechumenate.* Lydia, for example, was a catechumen. This ancient way of forming disciples is a means of welcoming and walking with those seeking faith and life with the church. Another way I describe the catechumenate is as a journey toward faith and baptism punctuated by ritual actions that mark the stages of formation and development. Today Roman Catholic, Episcopal, United Methodist, Mennonite, Presbyterian, Lutheran, and other churches are implementing this ancient-future way of forming Christians. Congregations are beginning to discover that people long for a deep spiritual journey that leads both to the bath and to full participation in worship and mission after they come up from it.

This journey to discipleship and strengthening of the whole community comes to focus in the Easter cycle. Lent and Easter combine the best evangelical and catholic instincts of the church. I like to think of this approach to formation as living on the porch—a porch is a public, open place to develop relationship through sharing our stories, feeling free to ask primary questions, and attending to the Word of God together. In short, it means doing the basics.[9] Aidan Kavanagh noted that a number of his students at Yale came to divinity school not because they were called to ordained or professional ministry but because they could not find the kind of deeply formative experiences they sought in the churches where they began their faith journeys. Perhaps you are reading this book because the Spirit seeks to form you more deeply in a life of prayer and faith.

- *Baptism is both a high moment and a daily grind.* Baptism and moments of repentance and renewal of the baptismal covenant can be and should be intense, emotional, and characterized by fire and flood, mystery and deep assurance. As Don E. Saliers notes in *Worship and Spirituality,*

> At the same time, living out our baptism into Christ means the manifestation of long-term passions for God and neighbor. Our love for God may itself have its ups and downs, fits and starts. But God's love for us is not dependent upon the ups and downs and fits and starts of human interiority.[10]

Maturity comes not with the intensity of our spiritual experiences but as the community lives toward conversion of its affections, desires, and practices of faith. "Living wet" reminds us that the pool of forgiveness and vocation is near.

Blessed are the churches where the font or pool is near the entrance so that we can experience anew the water and the Spirit. We are always starting over on this journey, and we travel with assurance of God's covenant promises made with us in baptism. The means of grace are not the "emotions of grace." They are the means of grace—divinely given ways of keeping our appointments with God in liturgy and life. They are the means of forming a lived practice of our baptismal covenant.

The depth of the baptismal journey is clear in Jesus' asking two disciples who had requested stations of privilege, "Are you able to . . . be baptized with the baptism that I am baptized with?" The question was rhetorical. "Then Jesus said to them, 'The cup that I drink you will drink; and with the baptism with which I am baptized, you will be baptized; but to sit at my right hand or at my left is not mine to grant, but it is for those for whom it has been prepared.'" (See Mark 10:35-40.) The false self wants to drive the Lexus and have a six-figure income, but Jesus calls us to pathways of sharing his baptism by letting go. He asks this of us so that we can be free to take up the cruciform life that points to the coming reign of God.

This baptism into Jesus' life calls for a steady practice of participating in the liturgy and living it out in daily decisions and relationships. Much of it is unseen and unsung by others, except those to whom we offer ourselves in acts of compassion and justice. We will often fail in living up to our baptismal promises to renounce evil and to repent of sin. Even though our old self drowns in baptism, it is a good swimmer! It takes a long time for our affections, tempers, and desires to let go and become the new self—a new creation in Christ.

If the font or baptismal pool is where you can get to it each time you enter the church, touch the water in some way that calls to your heart that you belong to God through baptism. In daily life, when you shower or bathe or drink a glass of water, call to mind your union with the church as the vanguard of witnesses to Love's new creation. Let baptismal consciousness shape your daily living.

QUESTIONS FOR REFLECTION

What stands out for you in this chapter and evokes your imagination? Spend time with that idea for a while, then enter into one of the following options. What emerges from it? Journal the questions, insights, and promptings of the Spirit.

Option 1: Imagine yourself in a worship service at your church. The font or pool is full of water, and the "flood prayer" (the Thanksgiving over the Water) is prayed; the pastor says, "Remember your baptism and be thankful." Everyone says, "Thanks be to God." Then the pastor invites people to come and touch the water.

As you move toward the water, what does baptism signify for you? How does it serve as a living spring for the way you live as a Christian? How does your life demonstrate a holiness that is ordinary and an identity that is extraordinary?

Option 2: Find a place where there is water, or take some water with you to your place of reflection. Fashion a cross of twigs or some other material. Read Mark 10:35-40. Brood over the connections between the sacramental experience of baptism and the "baptisms" of life that have taken place or will occur in your life. Record what comes to you in your journal.

Option 3: If you have an activist bent, go to some place of service and social ministry and participate in serving the poor or caring for the environment. As you engage in this time of ministry, connect this activity with your baptism. What awareness and insights come as you recall promising to renounce the spiritual forces of wickedness, repent of your sin in order to trust Jesus Christ with your life, and serve him in union with his church?

CHAPTER 5

The Rhythm of the Table:
Eucharistic Living

Throughout this book we have been working from the premise that liturgy is a deeply lived, public pattern of communal prayer. This understanding is especially important as we turn to Holy Communion, the Eucharist, the church's meal with the risen Christ.

In this chapter we will explore the roots and essential pattern of the Eucharist and discover how it becomes embedded in us as a pattern of communal life for daily ministry. We will attempt to envision a eucharistic piety that is both inward and personal and outward and social. In our culture, with its intense focus on the self, an intentional balance of the two is a contextually responsible part of discipleship and liturgical reflection.

RHYTHM AND PATTERN

Rhythm and pattern are essential to the performance and appreciation of music. It is difficult to imagine that totally random and atonal music would appeal to us. Upon hearing it, we might describe it as noise, but likely we would not call it music. Similarly, rhythm and pattern are essential to ordered Christian worship.

Perhaps while reading this book you've wondered: *Isn't that the downside of liturgy—that because of its repetitiveness and predictability, it can and often does become monotonous?* Yes, rhythm and pattern can be boring when too repetitive and unvarying. The kids' music piece "Chopsticks" is hardly a classic! It is easy but incredibly boring except for a little while when learning to play the piano or playing a musical game. The musical equivalent of graceful liturgy is not "Chopsticks" but something from Bach or the Beatles or Ray Charles! Liturgical worship without the Spirit's nuance, imagination, and depth is hardly what we are talking about.

During the last thirty years of the twentieth century, the church found much greater clarity about the essential pattern of worship on the Lord's Day. The overall pattern is Word *and* Table. While not all denominations require that each Sunday include both Word and Table, most ecumenical churches view Word and Table as the normative structure of Christian worship. We will look at the historic roots of this twin observance later in this chapter.

Two Patterns

Here I invite you to look with me at two patterns, one within the other: "the basic pattern" and "take, bless, break, and give." First, let's look at the *basic pattern of worship* used by many congregations today and see how it relates to the biblical patterns.

The overall structure of Word and Table consists of four movements. We will call it the basic pattern of Christian worship on the Lord's Day. The movements are these:

ENTRANCE

The people come together in the Lord's name. There may be greetings, music and song, prayer and praise.

PROCLAMATION AND RESPONSE

The Scriptures are opened to the people through the reading of lessons, preaching, witnessing, music, or other arts and media. Interspersed may be psalms, anthems, and hymns. Responses to God's Word include acts of commitment and faith with offerings of concerns, prayers, gifts, and service for the world and for one another.

THANKSGIVING AND COMMUNION

In services with Communion, the actions of Jesus in the Upper Room are reenacted:

> taking the bread and cup,
> giving thanks over the bread and cup,
> breaking the bread, and
> giving the bread and cup.

In services without Communion, thanks are given for God's mighty acts in Jesus Christ.

SENDING FORTH

The people are sent into ministry with the Lord's blessing.[1]

I like to think of this pattern of movements as something we humans can easily understand. Whenever we gather to feast and celebrate, we gather and greet one another. Then we tell stories and catch up on what has transpired since our last gathering. During this storytelling we respond as appropriate: laughing, crying, embracing, consoling, affirming, and promising to stay in touch or give support as needed. Then someone says, "Dinner's ready!" and we all gather around the table, affirming the host and giving thanks. We share food in ways that delight us and make us feel part of a special circle of family and friends. We rehearse central stories that constitute and form the family or group. We may sing songs. Then people yawn, exchange looks, and the sense prevails that it is time to end the gathering and go home. The host or hosts send everyone off with blessings that say, "Glad you came. Take care. See you soon."

That is what we do in the four movements of the basic pattern of worship! It is a human vehicle by which the risen Christ gathers and meets with his people Sunday by Sunday. We see this pattern quite clearly in Luke's telling of the two disciples journeying to Emmaus (24:13-35). The risen Christ meets the travelers; the scriptures are recalled and interpreted; a meal is set out and thanks given with sudden recognition of the One who is host; then they depart to tell of the encounter. Is Luke giving us the pattern of Lord's Day worship in this story? Or did the church as a community live into this pattern and recognize that from that first Easter its worship had a basic rhythm and order?

"Take, bless, break, and give": Now zoom in to the third movement of the basic pattern, *thanksgiving and communion*. In almost all accounts of his meals with others, both before and after the resurrection, Jesus demonstrates this fourfold action:

> He takes,
> he blesses God,
> he breaks,
> and he gives.[2]

We practice the same actions in Holy Communion. I want to focus on this fourfold action and then return to the four movements of the larger Word and Table pattern.

To appreciate Jesus' four actions in the Gospel food stories, I think it helps to look at a contrasting pattern that developed in the Garden of Eden. In Genesis 3 we read:

> The woman . . . *took of its fruit* and *ate*; and she also gave some to her husband, who was with her, and he ate. Then the eyes of both were opened, and they knew that they were naked; and they sewed fig leaves together and made loincloths for themselves.

> They heard the sound of the LORD God walking in the garden at the time of the evening breeze, and *the man and his wife hid themselves from the presence of the LORD God* among the trees of the garden. (vv. 6-8, emphasis added)

Here three actions occur in relationship to the fruit of the tree in the center of the Garden. The pattern of actions slightly differs from what Jesus characteristically did when taking the bread, but the results are oh so different! The ancient "threefold action" is simple and devastating to the creation: Adam and Eve took; they abused; and they hid from the Lord God. Imagine it. God had given them everything: "In love I made all of this for your enjoyment and stewardship. It is all available. Please enjoy it in my love. Just one thing over there is not good for you; indeed, you must not partake of it." But they did partake of it. The story starts as one of abundance and gracious availability. It ends with a pattern that is repeated in the corporate and political world and in our daily lives: we take; we break or abuse; and then we hide and make every effort to conceal what we have done. Where would Agatha Christie or any mystery writer be without this threefold action? Or how can we explain the devastation of families, the land, and various populations without being truthful about this pattern? Take, abuse, and hide.

Hold that pattern in mind, and let Matthew tell of the feeding of the multitude in chapter 14:

> Now when Jesus heard this [the beheading of John the Baptist], he withdrew from there in a boat to a deserted place by himself. But when the crowds heard it, they followed him on foot from the towns. When he went ashore, he saw a great crowd; and he had compassion for them and cured their sick. When it was evening, the disciples came to him and said, "This is a deserted place, and the hour is now late; send the crowds away so that they may go into the villages and buy food for themselves." Jesus said to them, "They need not go away; you give them something to eat." They replied, "We have nothing here but five loaves and two fish." And he said, "Bring them here to me." Then he ordered the crowds to sit down on the grass. *Taking the five loaves and the two fish*, he looked up to heaven, and *blessed* and *broke the loaves*, and *gave them* to the disciples, and the disciples gave them to the crowds. And all ate and were filled; and they took up what was left over of the broken pieces, twelve baskets full. And those who ate were about five thousand men, besides women and children. (vv. 13-21, emphasis added)

There it is, in stark contrast! Take, break, hide (the pattern of perceived scarcity) beside Jesus' pattern of take, bless, break, and give (the pattern of recognized abundance).

I don't want to oversimplify. Holy Communion is ever more deep and rich than one interpretive scheme. At the same time, we currently face ecological devastation and widespread poverty and deprivation around the world. Largely this is due to greedy, self-indulgent practices and economic patterns remarkably similar to the pattern begun in the Garden of Eden. This situation puts the Eucharist in a new light. Jesus replaces an old, destructive, narcissistic pattern with a new one.

Jesus' fourfold action, when rehearsed in the Eucharist, forms Christians in a new way of relating to the world. Is it too startling to think that in the liturgy and in the way we live out the liturgy in daily life, the world will recognize Christ?

This pattern—taking, blessing, breaking open, and giving—was so typical of Jesus' way at the table that on the day of resurrection, two travelers going toward Emmaus did not recognize him

By experiencing and sharing the Eucharist regularly through time, the church gets the new pattern into its neurons, muscles, and bones.

on the road, but when they were at table with him, they recognized him in the breaking of the bread (Luke 24:13-35). By experiencing and sharing the Eucharist regularly through time, the church gets the new pattern into its neurons, muscles, and bones. We shift from being a concealing people to a revealing people. We become transmitters of life, the life that is in Christ.

Communal liturgy *reveals* who Jesus is and who we are in relation to God. Communal liturgy also *transmits life*, the new life God gives us through Jesus Christ and which we then, with the guidance of the Holy Spirit, transmit to others. This pattern of worship comes from Jesus and is mediated to us through the early church's formation of ritual practice that had roots in Jesus' baptism, meal practices, and daily prayer.

It may help to review the origins of the sacrament of Holy Communion and how this ritual has been adapted and acculturated in many settings over time. I use *Holy Communion, Eucharist, Lord's Supper,* and *Holy Meal* interchangeably here because they are synonyms in the liturgical lexicon.

The Eucharist (from the Greek *eucharisteo,* meaning "to give thanks") has twin peaks—*service of the Word* and *service of the Table.* The roots of those two large movements come from worship practices in the synagogue and Temple and at the Jewish family table. Worship in the synagogue developed during the Jewish exile in Babylon following the destruction of the Temple. In the synagogue the Jews offered an "unbloody" sacrifice of reading the scriptures and prayer. These practices and worship ways were the precursors of our service of the Word. In the memory of the Temple and its reconstruction after the Exile, the Jews kept alive the "bloody" sacrificial practice by which they enacted their covenant relationship with God. The images and practices of this system were the precursors of our service of the Table. In addition, the Jews practiced family meal prayers of blessing God for the good gifts of providence. Taken together, these practices and pathways of prayer were familiar and observed by the first Christians, including Jesus.

In his meal practice Jesus was an observant Jew, but he "pushed the envelope." A boundary breaker, Jesus ate with sinners and fed the hungry. In doing so he broke open a closed religious and economic system and created life-giving pathways for repentance, inclusion, and holiness measured not by purity laws but by the way of love, justice, and participation in the bounty and abundance of God's in-breaking reign. In all the Gospel narrations where Jesus takes food and assumes the role of host at the table, he takes the bread/food, blesses God (in the manner of Jewish table prayer called *berekah*), breaks it open, and gives it in abundance as if there is enough for all the world. We see this same pattern in the synoptic Gospels (Matthew, Mark, and Luke) in the upper room the night before he was betrayed, which Christians point to and remember as the institution of the Lord's Supper. On the day of resurrection, we again see this pattern at the evening meal in Emmaus (Luke 24:13-35). In all these instances Jesus breaks barriers, and the Eucharist has from the start a connection with the radical incursion of God's reign.

The newly formed church (Acts 2) and what we call the New Testament church continued their meals with the risen Christ. Remember, the earliest Christians were Jews. They were thoroughly embedded in a Jewish matrix that included *Jewish formal meals*. These meals were real meals in the sense that the eucharistic feast included more than bread and wine. In 1 Corinthians 11 it is obvious that Paul is talking about a real meal when he criticizes those who rush ahead to eat while others are neglected in the sharing of food. Likely the meal was a version of the Jewish formal meal with a sevenfold pattern. At the beginning of the meal, the head of household (1) took bread, (2) offered a short blessing (*berekah*), (3) broke the bread, (4) shared it with all present, and (5) after the meal took a cup of wine, (6) said a longer blessing over it, and (7) shared it with all at the table.[3] While we do not know precisely how first-century eucharistic practice developed after the earliest scriptural accounts in 1 Corinthians 11 and the Gospel narratives of the upper room and Emmaus, we do have some clues.

Justin Martyr (c. 150 CE), writing to explain the practice of Christians in Rome, gives this extended description of their worship on Sundays:

On the *day which is called Sunday,* all who live in the cities or in the countryside *gather together* in one place. And the *memoirs of the apostles or the writings of the prophets are read* as long as there is time. Then, when the reader has finished, *the president, in a discourse, admonishes and invites the people to practice these examples of virtue.* Then *we all stand up together and offer prayers.* And, as we mentioned before, *when we have finished the prayer, bread is presented, and wine with water; the president likewise offers up prayers and thanksgivings* according to his ability, and *the people assent by saying, Amen. The elements which have been "eucharistized" are distributed and received by each one;* and *they are sent to the absent by the deacons.* Those who are prosperous, if they wish, contribute what each one deems appropriate; and the collection is deposited with the president; and he takes care of the orphans and widows, and those who are needy because of sickness or other cause, and the captives, and the strangers who sojourn amongst us—in brief, he is the curate of *all who are in need.* (emphasis added)[4]

This is a fascinating and illuminating passage. First, the *fellowship meal has disappeared,* and the sevenfold meal has become a fourfold action around the bread and cup (take, bless God, break the bread, give the bread and cup). Without the full meal between the bread and the cup, the two blessings were combined. Second, *something has been added.* Now *the meal is preceded by a service of readings, preaching, and intercessory prayer.* So, here in this early description we can see clearly what today we call the Word and Table shape of the Eucharist that combines the synagogue focus on the readings and interpretation with the temple and Jewish meal practices focused on the table. We don't know when this major change took place, but change it did. Third, we can see clearly the basic pattern or shape of the Sunday liturgy: gathering, proclamation and response, thanksgiving and communion, and going forth into the world of need.

There are several other notable features to the liturgy that Justin describes: (1) *Sunday* is identified as the day of gathering for the Eucharist. (2) *Various roles* have emerged, including *the president; readers; the congregation* standing for the prayers, offering the "Amen" at the end of the presider's thanksgivings, and receiving and communing in the bread and cup; and *the deacons'* sharing of Communion with those who were absent. (3) There is *a definite sense of community and belonging to one another.* Unlike what is often the case today, the congregation was a cohesive, interdependent, and closely linked body that noticed and looked after the absent and needy among them. (4) The congregation demonstrated *open-hearted compassion and a sense of just proportion* toward all who were in need. Justin writes, "Those who are prosperous, if they wish, contribute what each one deems appropriate; and the collection is deposited with the president." The Sunday gathering for the Eucharist had very real ethical connections to what the church did during its Monday-to-Monday living. Your church may continue this last practice by inviting congregants to give offerings for the needy as they come forward to receive Holy Communion.

The pattern Justin described has continued through the centuries, though often obscured by accretions (medieval elaborations), reduction of the assembly's participation (medieval and modernist periods), infrequent celebration in many eras (including Protestant America), obscuring (breaking up of the unity of the eucharistic prayer),[5] and an eclipse of the ethical connections between thanksgiving for God's richness toward us and "all who are in need." Thankfully, the liturgical movement's long struggle came to fruition in many denominations in the mid-1970s, and clarity about the overall basic pattern and the fourfold action at the table has been widely recovered. In the last thirty years, most Christian churches in North America have revised their worship books, and, in doing so, Christians are beginning to recover as normative the fullness of the ancient Word and Table pattern of worship and the fourfold table action.

How is it with your congregation and its practice of Word and Table? Does the service of the Word include a rich abundance: gathering, reading, interpreting scripture and life, telling the truth, interceding for the world and church, sharing the peace, and offering (as transition to the service of the Table)? Does the service of the Table incorporate setting out food, giving thanks, sharing, extending the table to the absent, communal generosity in caring for the needy, and sending the missionary community out into the world?

Eucharist in "Sorrow's Kitchen"

So, at the deepest levels, what takes place during the Holy Meal? What life-transforming dynamic occurs when your congregation celebrates the Lord's Supper? Perhaps we can helpfully imagine the Eucharist as spending time in "sorrow's kitchen."[6] The Eucharist is sorrow's kitchen, not only as sharing in eating the Paschal meal, which is an *anamnesis* of the dying and rising of Christ, but as sharing in the ambiguity and struggle of the world as it reflects the dying and rising of Christ. In sorrow's kitchen we mix the ingredients of our passage from death to life. We take, bless, break, and give the bread that is moistened with the world's tears, including our own. We add the flour of grain crushed and pulverized by the millstone of oppression, grief, and neglect. In other words, grateful celebration of the Eucharist finds a way to include and declare truthfully that life hurts. Passage from death to life, from sin to love, from living in the dark to living in the light, is painful.

Marx's charge that religion is the opium of the people is often all too true, but the Christian Eucharist ought never to be a numbing, pain-suppressing act. How can it be when the passage from death to life still continues in Iraq; in Jerusalem, the West Bank, and Gaza; in the Darfur region of Sudan; in the suffering of the poor in your city or county; in families living with Alzheimer's; in the abuse of children and the sex slave trafficking; and on and on? The Eucharist is "sorrow's kitchen" because it is where death and life meet each week. Here we partake of the realities of sickness, death, evil's bashing of the poor and marginalized, our complicity with wrong and harm (confession and pardon), and our own suffering and lament of injustice. We can do so because we proclaim Easter's faith: "Christ is risen from the dead, trampling down death by death, and on those in the tombs bestowing life!"[7] In the prayer book language we also proclaim Easter's ethical claim upon our lives when we declare, "Alleluia. Christ our Passover is sacrificed for us; therefore let us keep the feast. Alleluia."[8] (See 1 Cor. 5:7-8.)

Simple in elements and actions as the whole ritual is, sacramental worship becomes *telling the truth of the world's suffering and the mystery of God's love and victory in Christ.* That juxtaposition is potent and formative. The church's liturgy invites us to understand and enact that tension every Lord's Day. As Don E. Saliers puts it:

> If we are to have any sensible talk about Christian spirituality in our time, it must be refocused in the patterns

of our common liturgy, and we must learn again to be reconfigured in the baptismal pattern and the fourfold action around the altar. Such a way of life . . . cannot be understood or lived apart from the honest confrontation with suffering and mystery.[9]

He goes on to note that "most of the time human speech keeps us at a safe distance from the disorienting and painful features of our existence." We whine and moan, but it is a kind of safety valve that blows so we don't have to get in touch with the reality of evil powers, our complicity with them, and the suffering of the world. Contemporary culture is designed to keep us satiated and numb. Much of the time we participate in the liturgy of commodification and consumerism, salving our neediness, not with gospel play but with thinly veiled materialism and the narcissism of privilege. And so, as I noted earlier, "the liturgy waits for us." It waits for us to come home to God. It waits for us to let go of the pattern of scarcity and discover anew the pattern of abundance and faith.

What is God waiting to share with us? This question prompts in me the mental image of God hiding out at the table like a tiger waiting for us to enter the jungle of our own truth and God's mystery, waiting to capture us in Love's compelling paws. Christ the tiger is waiting to take us, bless God for us, break us open, and give himself to the world through us.

Part of what I want to get at here is the direction I think we must lean in celebrating Holy Communion. In the preaching, prayers of intercession, and the Great Thanksgiving, we must lean toward honest confrontation with suffering and mystery. Grace calls us toward this engagement with the ambiguity of "what is" in light of Christ's victory over sin and death. Here, in sorrow's kitchen, the liturgy invites our yearning for the full revelation of the sons and daughters of God and the fulfillment of the Paschal mystery that we affirm in the acclamation: "Christ has died; Christ is risen; Christ will come again." The Great Thanksgiving picks up the theme of victory and expresses our willingness to engage in the struggle and witness of living that takes place between Christ's dying and rising and Christ's final victory.

In a real sense the Eucharist vigorously protests the status quo by taking what is, blessing God for God's victory in Christ, letting ourselves be broken free of our isolation and self-absorption as we vow in baptism, and being given in union with Christ to be for the world the body of Christ, as we pray in the Great Thanksgiving. It is enacting an alternative to what is. It is playing on God's playground of hope and abundance. In this way the old pattern of take, break/abuse, and conceal is replaced each week (or each time we celebrate the Eucharist) by the new pattern of Christ's mercy and victory. Jacques Ellul would call this the combat of prayer, and Walter Wink would call it naming and engaging the powers. Orthodox Christians and a growing number of Christians in the West would call it *perichoresis*—sharing in and being taken up into the life of the Holy Trinity.[10]

The liturgy of Word and Table deeply forms a spirituality of truth telling, engaging with life in the world, opening to the ambiguity and mystery of life, and, increasingly, moving the community to a shared martyrdom among the poor and marginalized near and far. The Eucharist as the continuation of our baptism calls us to embrace our identity and ministry for the life of the world. How would this look in a particular setting? Here is one story.

After considerable study and reflection in the early 1980s, Broadway Christian Parish (United Methodist) in South Bend,

Indiana, decided to celebrate Holy Communion weekly. The congregation did not vote on making the weekly Eucharist normative but came to it as a discernment of God's call to them. They began on the first Sunday of Advent. The same day they also began serving a meal to the Broadway neighborhood. Unknown to the pastor, the laity had organized themselves into five meal teams. John Smith, the pastor at the time, told me, "This said to me they got it. The Eucharist was shaping their identity. They understood the connection between the sacraments and mission. It was as if they were saying, 'We've been fed; now we must feed others.'" Since that time this "near-death" congregation in the poorest part of the city has spread its fellowship hall tables with tablecloths, napkins, and nourishing food for all who would come from the community. The church sits down with the hungry ones of the neighborhood, enacting the grace of God given in baptism and nourished in the Holy Meal.[11] Might Justin have recognized his early-church practice in this present-day missionary community?

A kind of "white martyrdom"[12] grew in Broadway Christian Parish. A boy was killed in gunfire in the neighborhood. The next year, on Good Friday, members of the congregation walked the stations of the cross carrying a big wooden cross through the neighborhood. They walked to different places of hope and despair in the community, praying on the street where the boy was shot, in front of the drug houses, and other places where the ravages of poverty, racism, and suffering seemed to be having the final word. There they engaged in a kind of triumph song in the minor key: "Christ has died; Christ is risen; Christ will come again." The old pattern—take, abuse, conceal—may still raise its head and seem monstrously powerful, but the new pattern, enacted and embodied in baptism and the Eucharist, extends out into the world that we bring to God in prayer. "Alleluia. Christ our Passover is sacrificed for us; Therefore, let us keep the feast. Not with the old leaven of malice and evil, but with the unleavened bread of sincerity and truth. Alleluia."

"DO THIS"

In this chapter we have explored the rhythms and patterns (the basic fourfold order and the four actions at the table) of Holy Communion as a means of grace for shaping our living. The Holy Meal is an encounter with the risen Christ that changes our lives from living out of perceived shortage and patterns of greed to living out of God's abundance in patterns of communal prayer and deeds of compassion and justice. Perhaps the neglect of weekly Eucharist lies in our failure to see the deeply relevant connections of the sacrament to the way we live. Or, turning it around, maybe deep down we do see the connections and draw back from Holy Communion because partaking has consequences! Whatever the reasons for our holding back, Jesus says unequivocally, "Do this" (Luke 22:19). In celebrating Communion faithfully, regularly, and lavishly, we will discover what it means to take, bless, break open, and give ourselves to God and neighbor.

QUESTIONS FOR REFLECTION

1. What are your earliest memories of Holy Communion? Over the years how has your awareness of the meaning of Communion changed? In what ways do you see connections between the actions of the Eucharist and the ways you live in daily life and ministry? What connections do you make between the Eucharist and your life of prayer and other spiritual practices? Imagine your life shaped by take,

bless, break, and give as a pattern of prayer and action in sharing the heart, mind, and work of Christ.

2. What yearnings for enriched and more profound celebration of Holy Communion do you recognize in yourself and others in your congregation? How are you prompted to encourage and support more robust and transforming services of Word and Table in your church? How will you engage in prayer before and as you seek to influence changes in thinking and practice?

How Loud Should Liturgy Be?

F red Craddock once preached a sermon around the question, how loud should a sermon be? He preached it to a group of us pastors seeking refreshment for our weekly vocation of proclaiming the hope that holds and orients the community of faith. With grace and humor he got all of us thinking about how the tone and the intensity of preaching needed to match the context. For example, if it was Easter morning, we would proclaim the Resurrection in one way. If the occasion was the funeral of a five-year-old child, we would proclaim the Resurrection in another way. Shout the good news? Sometimes. Whisper it in hope? Sometimes. It is a matter of nuance and context.

Carry that over to the liturgy as a whole. How loud should the liturgy be? How solemn? How fast-paced? How measured? How formal? informal? How horizontal as Christians facing and addressing one another? How vertical as Christians beholding God and sharing in a rhythm of call-and-response with God? How engaging of the senses should the liturgy be? How emotional? How intellectual? How engaging of multiple intelligences? These questions and other similar ones take us into the deeper waters of what we have considered in this book. There are no categorically right answers to such questions.

Content and Context

Liturgical prayer is patterned communal actions around the strong center of Jesus Christ known through font, sacred stories, and faithful songs, table, seasons and festival days, and times of the day. The *content* of our liturgical prayer always has a context. While its outward form remains steady, the circumstances of our experience and the realities of our locality and the world's hurts and hopes affect the ways we participate and respond to God.

As illustration, take Peter's response to Jesus in two fishing stories (Luke 5 and John 21). In both instances, the "pattern" of the liturgy is the same: Peter and the disciples have been out fishing all night but have caught nothing. Jesus appears and tells them where to cast their nets. In each story Peter responds to Jesus, but the tone of Peter's response differs dramatically. In Luke 5, Peter responds to Jesus naively; he is amazed, moved, impressed, puzzled, and afraid because of the seemingly miraculous catch of fish, and Jesus as the mysterious captain of nature. In John 21, a post-Resurrection story, Peter responds to Jesus having had a history of relationship with him: he is eager, excited, in a dither! In one context, he wants Jesus to get *away* from him; in the other Peter is anxious to *get to* Jesus. How should liturgy *be*?

One decibel level and one intensity do not fit all situations in which we gather to worship God. We know this truth deep down, yet sometimes we allow ourselves to get in ruts rather than making the effort to sense how the Holy Spirit nudges us to move in the nuances of each gathering. Some congregations pray at level "ten" regardless of circumstances! Many assemblies treat the liturgical pattern as a checklist to get through, never slowing down to "breathe." I find such a pace exhausting. I want to call out, "Hey! Did you hear that? Could we have a moment to take it in; a moment to imagine, to wonder, to make some connections, to acknowledge our doubt?" Perhaps you have attended services where a scripture passage was read hurriedly, and then, without pause, a hymn was announced or another reading begun. How did you experience such a hurried sequence? Perhaps congregations get into such thoughtless ruts because the pastor-presider tends to lead with a booming voice that overpowers a sense of dialogue, or the congregation pays more attention to the clock than to the juxtaposition of images, actions, and words that invite attention, reflection, and digestion. Without moments of stillness and appreciative or pensive pauses, we rush on, and worship becomes a form of shouting. Is God hard of hearing? Is the Spirit in a hurry? A newcomer to some gatherings might draw that conclusion.

Early in the morning, most people get up and are relatively quiet until the house "wakes up." When a pedestrian steps into a crosswalk and doesn't see an oncoming car, we *shout*, "Look out!" This kind of sensitivity is essential to experiencing liturgical prayer. It has to be prayer with care for public communal enactment around font, book, table, times and seasons, and the context of these symbols here and now. It is a close reading of the heart: the inner condition of the community's heart, the hopes and hurts of the world's throbbing hearts, and a faithful awareness of the heart of God.

In liturgy we learn to pray—to live and speak in relationship to the God who welcomes, prompts, calls, hears, sees, attends, heals, feeds, restrains, liberates, and sends us to be where God goes ahead of us. This communal ritual prayer is our *vocation* and shapes us for enacting our vocation between liturgical gatherings.

In this book I have broadly outlined the ordered patterns of liturgical prayer and proposed connections for how prayer using these communal patterns guides our spirituality for daily living. In short, we have been seeking to attend to the ecology of worship—to how we are continually called to open ourselves to the interrelationship of all people and all life in God.

A Pilgrimage into the Life of God

Liturgical prayer invites us to pilgrimage and the grace suited to the stages of the journey. When we first discover the rich dimensions of liturgical prayer, we may be especially conscious, even fascinated, with the outward aspects of this way of worship. We like the art, architecture, shape, history, and sense of tradition that we experience. As time passes and this way of being together before God becomes more ingrained, we recognize that the Spirit is making connections between what we perceive in worship and what we are called to discern in our daily living. We may sense that we are spiraling deeper into the life of grace with recurring cycles of gospel, conversion, baptism (and periodic reaffirmations of the baptismal covenant), Eucharist, and mission in the world. We become ever more woven into the liturgy deeply lived. Farther along, we may discover that when we participate in the liturgy, we are caught up in mystery—the mystery of God's loving the world and the Paschal mystery as Love's dance—and that our lives are entwined with the life of the triune God, whose incarnation is the world.[1]

Orthodox theology (Eastern Christianity) calls this mysterious journey *divinization*—being taken up into the life of God, sharing in the life of God. This dynamic movement is also termed *perichoresis*—literally, "moving around" as in dancing. The three-in-one God is a community of love dancing with such mutual reverence for each other that this love spills over and reaches out to indwell us and to sweep us up into the life of God creating, redeeming, and sustaining the beloved. In this dance every person and all of creation is beloved. And God desires to indwell the creation with love until all is finally beloved by all of us.

Here we come to the heart of liturgical prayer: we find ourselves dancing with God! We become caught up in the mystery of Love's initiative and lose ourselves in God. As Charles Wesley put it, we are "lost in wonder, love, and praise."[2] Silence and wonder overtake our actions and words, and the only response is to be still in the midst of our reveling and rejoicing, or our lamenting and sorrowing, and yield to the still point of Love at the center of all that is. In the end liturgical prayer sweeps us up in the divine drama and apprehends us in Jesus Christ to live beyond anything we are capable of by ourselves. More and more the mind of Christ (Phil. 2:5) becomes part of the fabric of our very being.

The language of the liturgy becomes the basic grammar of our individual and communal orientation to the world. The movements and gestures of the liturgy become our body language in the cosmos. We are patterned by grace. We move from isolation to ever-widening awareness of relationship with the life of God in the whole creation—of God yearning for the beloved in ways that treasure, heal, renew, and sustain. Liturgical prayer takes us into depths of receiving, blessing, breaking open, and self-giving ever more imaginative, risky, and life releasing than we dare to conceive.

As you journey and participate in the church's public patterns of action, pay attention to promptings to be a lifelong learner. Read; reflect; welcome opportunities to study and inform your mind and heart about sacramental theology and liturgical practice. Since the *whole assembly*—both clergy and laity—worships God, none should excuse themselves from gaining greater clarity and appreciation for the ways *we* worship and keep our appointments with God.

In the end, whatever we can say about how liturgy patterns us, the primary shaping takes place in our encounter with God in embodying prayer around the central things. So, keep your appointments with God. Participate as fully as you can in the communal patterns of grace. Do so actively and consciously; then *let go* to be surprised by grace: simply rest in God and give yourself to whatever the Mystery has in store for the universe.

QUESTIONS FOR REFLECTION

1. Recall worship experiences when the tone and mood of the liturgy seemed inappropriate to the context. Then recall times when it was especially appropriate and fitting. What do you learn from your observations?

2. Thinking of the "ecology of worship," how do you live the connections between liturgical prayer and the life of the world? What practices will you adopt to see and make these connections in days to come?

3. What aspects of liturgy and liturgical prayer might you explore more fully? How will you do that—on your own or with others?

4. Imagine liturgy as a rope on which you can swing out over the "swimming hole" and let go. What comes to mind as you envision such a venture?

Group Study
and Exploration Guide

Individuals or groups can profit from reading this book. For individuals I have included suggestions for reflection at the end of each chapter.

In this section I offer suggestions for group interaction and reflection on the liturgy and participants' experience of it. These simple suggestions are intended to help group members enter into deeper dialogue with one another. A skilled leader will want to supplement these suggestions with approaches that are particular to the worship practices and liturgical style of the church or churches in which the participants worship.

Groups that can benefit from studying this book include

- adult Sunday school classes
- Lenten study groups
- worship commissions or worship teams
- church councils (possibly at a retreat or in preparation for yearly planning)
- groups meeting in residential centers, such as retirement homes

- lectionary study groups (clergy or lay)
- a class offered during a spiritual formation conference
- ecumenical (interdenominational) study groups

INTRODUCTION

1. Invite group members to share their first response to the word *liturgy*. Ask them to explain what past experience or lack of experience leads them to make such a response.

2. Ask participants to review the introduction and to name what in this exploration excites them.

3. Spend a little time discussing your group life for the weeks of this study. Clarify dates of group sessions, duration of each session, and any special activities or "field trip" experiences the group wants to build into the experience.

Assignment: Ask the group members to read chapter 1 for the next session and to journal their responses to "Reflecting on Your Experience of Liturgy" (p. 35).

CHAPTER 1   LITURGY AS BETHEL:
"THIS IS THE GATE OF HEAVEN"

1. Ask the group to respond to Marion's approach to loving God. Is it a new thought that a person could love God through the liturgy?

2. Invite group members to share their journaling around "Reflecting on Your Experience of Liturgy."

3. Look at the bulleted items under "Formative Dimensions of Liturgy" (p. 25 and following). Talk about which of these points each participant finds most illuminating for appreciating how worship shapes us. If the congregation under-

stood these dimensions, how might your church's worship and witness be strengthened?

4. In light of the section on pages 29–30 that compares tensions in the liturgy to the movement of tectonic plates, talk about how creative tensions are generated in the worship of your church. Are people aware of them? Welcoming or resistant to them? Do worshipers need opportunity to reflect on and talk about their experience in order to appreciate and grow as a result of creative tension in the liturgy?

5. Ask one person to read aloud the prayer at the end of chapter 1 as the rest of the group listens and makes it their prayer.

Assignment: Ask the group to read chapter 2 for next week. If there is a cathedral church, monastery, or convent nearby where the daily office is prayed, invite participants to share in that community's public prayer. If possible, go as a group.

CHAPTER 2   DAILY PRAYER WITH THE CHURCH: THE DAILY OFFICE

1. Invite participants to share their favorite time of day and what makes it significant to them. What responses of appreciation or delight do individuals make to that time of day? How do they invest themselves in it? Does connecting that time of day with acts of praise and prayer make sense to them?

2. Ask, "How do you respond to the practice of prayer at certain times of the day as a communal act?" Welcome and accept negative as well as positive responses. Discuss the pros and cons of such a practice. To give focus, you might list them on newsprint or chalkboard. Draw upon material

in the chapter regarding daily communal and private prayer. If any in the group participated in the daily office at a monastery or cathedral church during the preceding week, invite those persons to talk about their experience.

3. If your group meets in the early morning, near noon, or at evening, consider praying the daily office for that time of day. Use an order from your denomination's worship book (or some other, such as the Book of Common Prayer or *Upper Room Worshipbook*). Plan which hymn(s), psalm(s), scripture reading(s), and prayers you will use. Keep the service fairly simple, and create or go into a space that is conducive to prayer. You could open or close the session with this prayer service.

4. Discuss the history of the daily office and the different patterns (monastic and cathedral) that developed. Consider which pattern better suits the spirituality and lifestyle of people in your congregation.

5. The chapter refers to childhood and youth experiences such as the bedtime prayer "Now I lay me down to sleep" and campfire vespers. Invite the group to recall similar experiences in their lives and to name others that shape their sense of spiritual connection with communal prayer at sunrise, midday, evening, and night. You might begin this part with an invitation to journal or silently recall these memorable occasions and then to share aloud. This will give introverts the time and space they need for reflection.

6. Invite participants to review in silence the section "How Daily Prayer Stretches Our Experience of Communal Prayer," pages 48–55. Ask group members to focus on one

practice that tugs at them the most and to imagine themselves making time for that practice at least once each day with a sense of relationship to the whole church's prayer.

7. List the bulleted items under "Getting Started," pages 55–57. Invite individuals to share which of these approaches they believe would most help them to begin a practice of praying the daily office.

8. Close the session with a prayer suited to the time of day. (See "The Daily Office" in the Book of Common Prayer, or consult another book listed in the chapter.) Allow time for silence after the prayer to give opportunity for any who are so prompted to give thanks or express some commitment to practicing daily prayer.

9. Consider viewing one or more segments of the DVD in Robert Benson's book *Daily Prayer*. (See "Selected Bibliography," p. 155.)

Assignment: Ask group members to read chapter 3 for the next session and reflect on the questions at the end of the chapter. Ask one person to find information about the *Revised Common Lectionary* (RCL) and make a brief report to the group at the next meeting. Invite this participant to go to www.commontexts.org, the Consultation on Common Texts Web site, and to review your denomination's worship book to see what it says, if anything, about the RCL.

CHAPTER 3   CYCLES IN TIME:
THE CHRISTIAN YEAR AND SPIRITUALITY

1. Light a candle and offer a prayer appropriate to the current season of the church year. Your denomination's hymnal or

worship book will be a good source. Or you could build on last week's exploration and lead a simple service of morning or evening prayer, depending on the time of day, that includes reference to the season.

2. Turn to the chart of "The Liturgical Year" on page 71 and play with the notion that by following the church year, we tell the story of Jesus Christ. Ask for a volunteer to start the "storytelling" by choosing one of the seasons and saying, "In _____ (naming the season or festal day) we tell of _____." Then that person can say, "And . . ." and someone else picks up the storytelling by saying, "And in _____ we tell of _____." Continue until each season or special day is covered in this way.

3. Have the person who researched the *Revised Common Lectionary* share discoveries with the group.

4. Look at your church's order of service and talk about the concept of *anamnesis* (see pp. 67 and 149) as remembering the past so that it becomes present and real. When in your worship service does this remembrance happen most vividly? What could be done to strengthen this sense of our being present to Christ and his being present to us?

5. When we think of spiritual formation, we often associate it with being centered, quiet, prayerful. This chapter talks about "dangerous" liturgy (p. 67) and how telling the story using the calendar and lectionary leads us to transcend the comfortable boundaries of time and space. In what sense is the liturgy dangerous to us? to our false self? In what ways has the liturgy reoriented or shaped your sense of prayer and commitment?

6. If your group is meeting during the season of Lent, consider planning to attend an Easter Vigil service in your community. Plan to reflect on the experience together immediately after the vigil or at the next group session.

7. Discuss cycles in time. What do we love about preparation, celebration, returning to the ordinary? Why do we resist cycles and rituals of celebration? How do cycles and seasons enable Christian growth—in other words, in what ways do they shape and reshape us more and more to a cruciform way of living? What clues does the hymn quoted at the beginning of chapter 3 give?

Assignment: Ask participants to read chapter 4 for the next session and to reflect on the questions at the end of the chapter. If the group is interested, invite members to bring something that connects them to their baptisms, such as a photo, baptismal certificate, or a gift received upon baptism.

CHAPTER 4   BY WATER AND THE SPIRIT: LIVING OUT OUR BAPTISM

1. Ask individuals to share what surprised them or stirred them in "Easter in Ephesus." Does the story evoke a desire for more significant baptismal celebrations? Or not? How does the group feel about the author's assertion that much of present-day baptism and Holy Communion practice suffers from minimalism? (See p. 86.)

2. Place a bowl of water in the center of the group. Ask the group to imagine the font or pool in your church and hold that in mind, remembering their baptisms and the baptisms of others, both young and old, and then to say several times in unison, "This is our bathtub, our fountain of life."

This exercise might feel a little silly and playful. Discuss the feelings and the deeper dimensions of what it means that we have a common bath and fountain.

3. How well do you and your congregation live attentively to the Spirit in all relationships and situations? Do congregational prayers and preaching give witness to the places where God is doing a new thing in the midst of the pain and struggle for peace and justice? In what ways do you connect the renunciation and profession of the rite of baptism with living a disciplined spirituality with other members of the body of Christ?

4. Ask the group to reread "Baptism is both a high moment and a daily grind" on page 99. Talk about the means of grace. (See the John Wesley quotation on p. 19 and the paragraph beginning "Maturity comes not with the intensity of our spiritual experiences . . ." on p. 99.) As a first step, the group may find it helpful to list as many of the means of grace (see glossary on p. 152) as they can. Then talk together about how the means of grace and holding one another accountable for their use is critical to connecting our baptismal vows with the "daily grind." Are there ways this group would be willing to covenant to stay in touch for the use of the means of grace and keeping faith with their renunciation of evil and sin and continuing to love and serve Christ?

Assignment: Ask the group to read chapter 5 and to reflect on the questions at the end of the chapter.

CHAPTER 5   THE RHYTHMS OF THE TABLE:
EUCHARISTIC LIVING

1. Place a loaf of bread on a table in the center of the group.
   If your session will conclude with a service of Holy Communion (see suggestion 7, p. 137), have whatever the presiding minister recommends—at least bread, a cup of
   grape juice or wine, and a laundered and pressed cloth.

2. Ask each group member to find a partner and share his or
   her earliest memory of Holy Communion and what it
   meant back then. After a few minutes, invite the pairs to
   come back together to share with the entire group.

3. Tell the group members to listen for a word or phrase that
   stands out for them as someone reads aloud Genesis 3:6-9.
   After the reading, pause for at least one minute; then ask,
   "What word or phrase stood out for you in this passage?"
   Without discussion, ask each participant to say in turn the
   word or phrase. Then ask someone else to read the same
   text again as everyone ponders the question, "What does
   this passage say about us as human beings and our situation?" Allow at least a minute of silence; then invite individuals to share in response to their deeper listening to the
   story without comment from other group members. Have
   a third member read the text again, asking the group to listen with this question in mind: "What does this say about
   God?" Allow at least a minute or two of silence; then invite
   each person to share, again without comment from other
   members of the group.

4. Ask the group to discuss the two contrasting patterns
   related to scarcity and abundance: take, break/abuse, and
   conceal next to take, bless, break open, and share. Does the

group agree that repetition of the eucharistic pattern can transform how we live our daily lives? What would have to change in your congregation and in its understanding and practice to lead to eucharistic living? How does Justin Martyr's description (p. 112) illuminate eucharistic congregational life?

5. Invite group members to share their journaling or musings on the second set of questions at the end of chapter 5. Listen carefully and draw out the feelings and convictions that are shared. Do you hear some common concern or prompting? Reflect it back to the group, seeking to help participants discern if there is a pathway they are willing to walk for the sake of deep communion with God in celebrating the Eucharist.

6. In the section "Eucharist in Sorrow's Kitchen" (p. 114ff.) the author leans toward sacramental celebration that connects our praise-filled celebration of Christ's victory with the mystery and ambiguity of life, particularly the suffering and struggle of others, as well as our own. Encourage individuals to share feelings and convictions about this approach to the Lord's Supper. Discuss these questions:

   • In what sense does God wait for us in the liturgy? in the pain and need of the world?

   • Are we willing and ready to come to the table of Christ the tiger?

   • Are we willing to be taken, blessed before God, broken open in compassion and justice, and be the means by which God gives Godself to the world?

7. If an authorized or ordained person is present or willing to come for this part of the session, celebrate the Lord's Supper together. Be sure to use the fourfold action at the table and use a full prayer of Great Thanksgiving. If no one is available to preside, the group can celebrate the experience of being together in learning and formation by joining hands and inviting any who wish to offer prayers of thanksgiving and petition. Conclude by singing the Doxology, "Praise God, from Whom All Blessings Flow."

Assignment: Ask the group to read the "Postscript" and respond to the questions that follow it.

POSTSCRIPT: HOW LOUD SHOULD LITURGY BE?

1. Discuss ways your congregation pays attention to the "context" of its liturgical life and worship. How does liturgy in your church attend to the hurts, struggles, and hopes of the world? the earth and its ecosystems? the people in the local community, especially the needy or the marginalized? Discuss specific instances that participants can recall and how this attention was enacted in the liturgy.

2. Thinking about the course of the church calendar, talk about the different moods of the various seasons and special days, and what liturgical actions and practices evoke the tone and moods of worship. See the chart on page 71 as a reminder of the full range of the liturgical year.

3. Invite participants to reread the first paragraph of the section "A Pilgrimage into the Life of God," page 124. Ask them to share where they see themselves on the pilgrimage described by the author and what the prospect of their being "ever more woven into the liturgy deeply lived" and

"caught up in mystery—the mystery of God's loving the world" evokes in them.

4. On page 126 the author urges continuing the journey in active and "resting" ways. Invite group members to list some ways they can continue to be learners in relationship to the church's liturgy. On the other side, "resting," ask, "Does letting go to be surprised by grace come with more or less difficulty for those who have studied and reflected deeply on sacramental theology and liturgy?"

5. If you as leader sense that participants yearn for more richly liturgical worship in their church, invite them to talk about what they long for in worship. List these for all to see. Brainstorm possible steps participants could take to fulfill their longing, both by supportive actions within the congregation and, if necessary, by occasionally participating in the worship of other congregations or communities whose worship more nearly approximates what they yearn for. As best you can, keep the conversation positive and grounded in their sense of the Spirit's empowerment. Avoid descending into frustration and feelings of powerlessness. Someone said, "There is no such thing as a bad day (or church) if there is a doorknob on the inside." Lead this discussion prayerfully.

6. Assuming this is the last group session, spend a few minutes discussing three questions:

   • What was the best thing about this group experience for you? (List responses on newsprint or a chalkboard.)

   • What would have made this study a better experience? How could it be improved? (List the responses.)

- How have you/we been shaped by this journey together? (List the responses.)

Consider whether to share any of the responses to the third question with the pastor or congregation and how best to do so.

7. Close with a time of prayer, perhaps using prayers from the daily office or from the Christian year. Allow for times of silence, and invite participants to offer prayers of thanksgiving or petition for the local church, one another, deepening the practice of living the liturgy, and other prayers as the Spirit prompts them. Finally, enact a blessing and sending forth of the group. See your church's hymnal or book of worship for possible texts, but feel free to adapt what you find to the context of this moment in the group's life.

Notes

Introduction

1. Albert C. Outler, ed., "The Means of Grace" in *The Works of John Wesley*, vol. 1 (Nashville: Abingdon Press, 1984), 396.

Chapter 1   Liturgy as Bethel:
"This is the Gate of Heaven"

1. Don E. Saliers, *Worship and Spirituality*, 2nd ed. (Akron, OH: Order of Saint Luke Publications, 1996), 59.

2. Erik Erikson, *Toys and Reasons: Stages in the Ritualization of Experience* (Toronto: McLeod, 1972), 49.

3. Gordon W. Lathrop, *Holy Things: A Liturgical Theology* (Minneapolis: Fortress Press, 1993), 174–76.

4. Saliers, *Worship and Spirituality*, 33.

5. See Lathrop, *Holy Things*, 33–83.

6. *The Revised Common Lectionary: The Consultation on Common Texts* (Nashville: Abingdon Press, 1992). This volume provides the calendar and tables of readings for Years A, B, and C keyed to the respective Gospel: Matthew for Year A, Mark for Year B, and Luke for Year C.

7. Several lectionaries containing services of daily prayer are available: Book of Common Prayer (New York: Church Hymnal Corporation and Seabury Press, 1977); *The Book of Common Worship, Daily Prayer* (Louisville, KY: Westminster John Knox Press, 1994); Mark Wesley Stamm, ed., *The Daily Lectionary: A Book of Hours for Daily Prayer*, vol. 6, The Daily Office Series (Akron, OH: Order of Saint Luke Publications, 2001); *Lutheran Book of Worship* (Minneapolis: Augsburg Publishing House, 1978); and *Revised Common Lectionary Daily Readings: Consultations on the Common Texts* (Minneapolis: Augsburg Fortress, Publishers, 2005).

CHAPTER 2   DAILY PRAYER WITH THE CHURCH:
THE DAILY OFFICE

1. From "The Great Thanksgiving," in "A Service of Word and Table I," *The United Methodist Hymnal* (Nashville: United Methodist Publishing House, 1989), 10. This expression of our sacrifice of praise and thanksgiving in union with Christ's offering for us recurs in all of the United Methodist prayers of Great Thanksgiving except the one in "A Service of Word and Table IV."

2. See the Book of Common Prayer; *The Book of Common Worship, Daily Prayer; Lutheran Book of Worship*; The Order of Saint Luke's *The Daily Office*, vols. 1–6; *Upper Room Worshipbook: Music and Liturgies for Spiritual Formation*. Additional options are available online. Search Daily Office, Liturgy of the Hours, and Daily Prayer for starters.

3. By "spiritual readings" I mean any nonbiblical text that aims to focus our spirits on God and deepen God's grasp of us, interpreting us to ourselves. Any of the great classical to contemporary spiritual writers—from the desert fathers and mothers to Evelyn Underhill to Henri Nouwen—could be used. A useful collection of such readings is Rueben P. Job and Norman Shawchuck's *A Guide to Prayer for All Who Seek God* (Nashville: Upper Room Books, 2003).

4. Source unknown. Some question the appropriateness of this prayer for children. An alternate version adds or substitutes two lines:

> May God guard me through the night
> And wake me with the morning light.

5. English Language Liturgical Consultation, *Praying Together* (Nashville: Abingdon Press, 1988), 53.

6. Thomas Merton, *Bread in the Wilderness* (Collegeville, MN: The Liturgical Press, 1971), 61.

7. You can find daily lectionary readings in the Book of Common Prayer, 933ff.; *The Book of Common Worship, Daily Prayer,* 459ff.; *The Daily Lectionary: A Book of Hours for Daily Prayer,* vol. 6, The Daily Office Series (Akron, OH: Order of Saint Luke Publications, 2001); and *Revised Common Lectionary Daily Readings: Consultations on the Common Texts.*

8. *Lesser Feasts and Fasts 2003* (New York: Church Publishing, 2003) and Clifton F. Guthrie, ed., *For All the Saints: A Calendar of Commemorations for United Methodists* (Akron, OH: Order of St. Luke Publications, 1995).

9. For more daily office resources and orders of service and prayers, go to:

- www.oremus.org
- www.missionstclare.com
- www.northumbriacommunity.org/Pray the Office/indexhtml
- www.dailyoffice.org

There are many more Web sites. Explore these and others to find what suits your style and needs.

10. From "The Day Thou Gavest, Lord, Is Ended," *The United Methodist Hymnal,* no. 690. Words by John Ellerton, 1870.

CHAPTER 3   CYCLES IN TIME:
THE CHRISTIAN YEAR AND SPIRITUALITY

1. From "O Love, How Deep," *The United Methodist Hymnal,* no. 267. Words from fifteenth-century Latin; trans. Benjamin Webb, 1854; altered.

2. Some churches have begun to include a season of creation in their liturgical calendar. Time will tell whether this season wins

broad acceptance in many churches and so reshapes the calendar. For more information about the season of creation, go to:

www.seasonofcreation.com/index.asp.

3. See chapters 30–49 in *Egeria: Diary of a Pilgrimage*, trans. George E. Gingras, Ancient Christian Writers series, no. 38 (New York: Newman Press, 1970) and F. L. Cross, ed., *St. Cyril of Jerusalem's Lectures on the Christian Sacraments: The Procatechesis and the Five Mystagogical Catecheses* (Crestwood, NY.: St. Vladimir's Seminary Press, 1977).

4. For more on the early development of this story, see *The Awe-Inspiring Rites of Initiation: The Origins of the RCIA*, 2nd ed. by Edward Yarnold (Collegeville, MN: Liturgical Press, 1994) and chapter 6 in *Come to the Waters: Baptism and Our Ministry of Welcoming Seekers and Making Disciples* by Daniel T. Benedict Jr. (Nashville: Discipleship Resources, 1996).

5. Per Harling, ed., *Worshipping Ecumenically: Orders of Service from Global Meetings with Suggestions for Local Use* (Geneva: WCC Publications, 1995), 5.

6. *The Constitution on the Sacred Liturgy of the Second Vatican Council and Motu Proprio of Pope Paul VI* (Glen Rock, NJ: Paulist Press, 1964), 36. This phrase, "full, conscious, and active participation," has been widely used by Catholic and Protestant liturgical leaders as a manifesto of what must characterize vital and faithful Christian worship.

7. See *On Common Ground: The Story of the Revised Common Lectionary* by Horace T. Allen Jr. and Joseph P. Russell (Norwich: Canterbury Press, 1998). Unfortunately, this book is out of print. For a short background of the Revised Common Lectionary, go to:

www.commontexts.org

8. Susan J. White, *The Spirit of Worship: The Liturgical Tradition* (London: Darton, Longman and Todd, 1999), 69.

9. Ibid.

10. From "Jesus Calls Us," *The United Methodist Hymnal*, no. 398. Words by Cecil Frances Alexander, 1852.

11. From "A Service of Word and Table I," *The United Methodist Hymnal*, 6.

12. For the text of the Exsultet, see the Book of Common Prayer, 286–87; *The Book of Common Worship*, 300–303; Hoyt L. Hickman et al., *The New Handbook of the Christian Year* (Nashville: Abingdon Press, 1992), 194–95; *The United Methodist Book of Worship*, 371–72; or *The Worship Sourcebook* (Grand Rapids, MI: CRC Publications, 2002), 631–33.

13. See Thomas J. Talley, *Origins of the Liturgical Year* (Collegeville, MN: Liturgical Press, 1986), parts 2 and 3.

14. See Paul F. Bradshaw, *Early Christian Worship: A Basic Introduction to Ideas and Practice* (Collegeville, MN: Liturgical Press, 1996), 88–89.

CHAPTER 4   BY WATER AND THE SPIRIT:
LIVING OUT OUR BAPTISM

1. This phrase comes from a classic definition of the sacraments in the catechism of the Book of Common Prayer, page 857. The full sentence reads: "Q: What are the sacraments? A: The sacraments are outward and visible signs of inward and spiritual grace, given by Christ as sure and certain means by which we receive that grace."

2. In the case of infant baptism, the response on the part of the person being baptized will necessarily come later. The congregation expresses its faith in the rite and anticipates a day when the newly baptized will be able and prepared to profess the faith of the church for themselves. See *By Water and the Spirit: Making Connections for Identity and Ministry* by Gayle C. Felton (Nashville: Discipleship Resources, 1997), particularly pages 1–5, 9–13, and 27–31.

3. See Baptismal Covenants I, II, and IV in *The United Methodist Hymnal*, pages 33, 39, and 50.

4. From *The Book of Common Worship* (Louisville, KY: Westminster John Knox Press, 1993), 404–5.

5. These services of reaffirmation of the baptismal covenant are sometimes included as part of a service when candidates are baptized, con-

firmed, or received into membership. Some congregations use the services when there are no candidates, especially on Easter, Pentecost, All Saints' Day, and Baptism of the Lord. For ritual texts for these services of reaffirmation, see the Book of Common Prayer, pages 292–94 and 309–10; *The Book of Common Worship*, pages 442–44, 464–71, and 485–88; *Evangelical Lutheran Worship* (Minneapolis: Augsburg Fortress Press, 2006), pages 234–37; *The United Methodist Hymnal*, pages 37 (nos. 12–13) and 50–53.

6. The Greek word for fish, *ichthus*, and the representation of a fish held significant meaning for early Christians. The letters ICHTHUS served as a brief acrostic profession of faith: *Iesous* (Jesus) *CHristos* (Christ) *THeou* (God) *Uios* (Son) *Soter* (Savior). All those who professed this faith in this great fish were themselves "little fishes," according to the well-known passage of Tertullian ("On Baptism," chapter 1): "But we, little fishes, after the example of our Ichthus, Jesus Christ, are born in water."

7. Many Lutheran, Episcopal, and Catholic churches celebrate the Easter Vigil; increasingly Presbyterian, United Church of Christ, and United Methodist churches are recovering the practice. You can find the rubrics and texts of the Easter Vigil in a number of sources: *The New Handbook of the Christian Year*, the Book of Common Prayer, *The United Methodist Book of Worship*, and *The Book of Common Worship*.

8. Book of Common Prayer, 286–87.

9. For an exploration and proposed implementation of this ancient-future way of making disciples, see Benedict, *Come to the Waters*. Also visit www.catechumenate.org.

10. Saliers, *Worship and Spirituality*, 54.

CHAPTER 5   THE RHYTHMS OF THE TABLE:
EUCHARISTIC LIVING

1. See "The Basic Pattern of Worship" in *The United Methodist Book of Worship*, 15. These headings are also those used in *The United Methodist Hymnal*, 2. Other churches use similar language to describe this basic pattern of worship. The amazing and fortuitous reality is that there is broad appreciation and acceptance of the basic pattern in Roman Catholic and ecumenical Protestant churches.

2. See the following "food stories," where this fourfold action is clearly evident: Matthew 14:13-21; 15:32-39; 26:26-30; Mark 6:35-44; 8:1-10; 14:22-25; Luke 9:12-17; 22:14-20; 24:28-35; John 6:1-14. Note that in the John text, the action of breaking is not explicit, though it is implied.

3. For more on Jewish formal meals and the development of the Eucharist, see chapter 6 in Dennis E. Smith, *From Symposium to Eucharist: The Banquet in the Early Christian World* (Minneapolis: Fortress Press, 2003).

4. Justin Martyr, "The First Apology of Justin Martyr," in *Liturgies of the Western Church*, ed. Bard Thompson (Cleveland, OH: William Collins Publisher, 1961), 9. Currently published by Augsburg Fortress Publishers.

5. A recent example of this breaking up of the unified prayer can be found in "The Order for the Administration of the Sacrament of the Lord's Supper" in *The Book of Worship for Church and Home* (Nashville: Methodist Publishing House, 1964), 19–22. The historic Anglican texts in these "prayers" were again unified in "Word and Table IV" in *The United Methodist Hymnal* (1989) and *The United Methodist Book of Worship* (1992). See respectively pages 27–31 and 46–49.

6. I borrow this phrase from Mary E. Lyons's *Sorrow's Kitchen: The Life and Folklore of Zora Neale Hurston* (New York: Scribner's, 1990).

7. From the Orthodox liturgy for Easter.

8. Based on 1 Corinthians 5:7-8; from the Book of Common

Prayer, 364. The ethical connection between our feasting with Christ and our mission in the world could be strengthened by including the rest of the text: "not with the old yeast, the yeast of malice and evil, but with the unleavened bread of sincerity and truth."

9. Saliers, *Worship and Spirituality*, 58.

10. See Jacques Ellul, *Prayer and Modern Man*, trans. C. Edward Hopkins (San Francisco: HarperSanFrancisco, 1973); Walter Wink, *The Powers That Be: Theology for a New Millennium* (New York: Doubleday, 1998); Catherine Mowry LaCugna, *God for Us: The Trinity and Christian Life* (San Francisco: HarperSanFrancisco, 1991); and C. Baxter Kruger, *The Great Dance: The Christian Vision Revisited* (Vancouver, BC: Regent College Publishing, 2005).

11. This narrative is based on an interview with the Rev. John E. Smith, who served as pastor of the congregation at the time of this development in Broadway Christian Parish. The incident of the shooting of the boy and the public praying of the stations of the cross event occurred after John was appointed to another church. Name and story used with permission.

12. *Red martyrdom* means losing one's life in witness and service for Christ. In the early church and periodically through history, Christians have been killed because of their faith. By contrast, *white martyrdom* indicates a person's abandoning safety and the false self for the sake of God and God's mission. The early desert fathers and mothers, the monastics, missionaries, and many ordinary people live as white martyrs.

POSTSCRIPT: HOW LOUD SHOULD LITURGY BE?

1. See Sallie McFague, *The Body of God: An Ecological Theology* (Minneapolis: Fortress Press, 1993), and *Life Abundant: Rethinking Theology and Economy for a Planet in Peril* (Minneapolis: Fortress Press, 2001) for a thorough exploration of the connection of the life of God with the life of the cosmos.

2. "Love Divine, All Loves Excelling" is found in many hymnals, including *The United Methodist Hymnal*, no. 384.

GLOSSARY

The meanings of the terms in this glossary are not necessarily the classic and technical definitions of these words. For those, readers should check more definitive sources. The following are working definitions for readers of this book.

Anamnesis—a peculiarly Jewish-Christian "think-thank" or "retell-thank" practice of remembering and representing God's grace-filled actions in the past in such a way as to experience their reality and immediacy in the present. This Greek word can only be approximated in English by such words as *remember, represent, recall,* and *experience anew.* The key instance of this word in Luke and Paul's writings is "Do this in *anamnesis* of me" (Luke 22:19; 1 Cor. 11:24-25)—a text included in the Great Thanksgiving at the Eucharist.

Assembly—the local gathering of those God has called to gather around font, book, and table as a community of prayer and praise to God. In the New Testament the Greek word *ekklesia* (literally "called" and "out") occurs over one hundred times and is often translated as "church." Originally it referred to a convocation or political assembly of citizens. Early Christians used it to refer to the assembly of Christians gathered for worship and mission. As a local community or congregation, the assembly embodies the whole (catholic/universal) church in this particular locality.

Daily Office— Sometimes referred to as daily prayer or the divine office, this is a historic practice of communal singing or recitation of the Psalms, reading the scriptures, and saying or singing canticles and prayers at set times of the day. While the monastic tradition prays seven offices each day, the primary form of the daily office for nonmonastic Christians includes Morning Prayer and Evening Prayer with shorter offices for noon and bedtime (compline). See chapter 2, where daily prayer is considered in depth.

Eighth day of creation—This phrase is a poetic reference to Easter and God's re-creation of all things, starting with the resurrection of Jesus Christ, as Paul proclaims in 1 Corinthians 15. See verses 20-28. The image presumes the Jewish story that God created in six days and "rested on the seventh day from all the work [God] had done" (Gen. 2:2). Christians baptized into Christ live in and into the coming reality of the "eighth day" of creation—that is, the consummation of all things in God.

Evangelical (adjective)—*Evangelical* refers to understandings and practices that communicate and embody the hope and life available in Christ. While in contemporary North American usage (and other parts of the world) *evangelical* has come to be associated with a narrow and often ideological agenda of the Christian right, in this book the meaning and use refers to the "good news," especially as embodied in the life and ministry of Jesus Christ (see Mark 1:1) and narrated in the four canonical Gospels.

Feast (as in Feast of the Resurrection)—In liturgical understanding and practice, there are "feasts" and "fasts" in the seasons and special days of the Christian calendar. Feast days and seasons are festive occasions celebrating God's mighty acts (Easter, Christmas, Pentecost, Ascension, All Saints' Day, etc.). Fasts are occasions of repentance or disciplined preparation, such as Advent, Ash Wednesday, Lent, Holy Week, etc. All Sundays of the year are "little" Easters, even in Lent.

Juxtaposition (in liturgy)—the dynamic interaction of tensions or polarities in the liturgy that results in or reveals something new, just as tectonic plates pushing against each other create mountains ranges and other geologic changes. Examples in worship include Sunday next to other days of the week, praise next to lament, Word next to Table, Easter next to (the rest of the) year, individual next to community, present reality next to "not-yet" but promised future, etc.

Lectionary—a table of Bible readings appointed for use on Sundays and special days of the Christian year. Lectionaries have been used by churches throughout Christian history. Present-day lectionaries include *The Lectionary for Mass* (Roman Catholic) and the *Revised Common Lectionary* (used by many Anglican and Protestant denominations around the world). Both are three-year systems of reading the Bible with three readings for each Sunday or special day: an Old Testament reading (with an appointed psalm as response), an Epistle reading, and a Gospel reading. Each of the three years is keyed to a different synoptic Gospel (Year A—Matthew, Year B—Mark, Year C—Luke) with readings from the Gospel of John interspersed through each of the three years. For more detail go to www.commontexts.org.

Means of grace—the practices or spiritual disciplines ("instituted" by Christ or tried-and-true practices, called "prudential") by which Christians keep their appointments with God and open themselves to experience God's sanctifying grace and presence. The means of grace include praying (personal and communal), reading scripture, attending worship weekly, participating in Holy Communion, "doing no harm, doing good," and so forth.

Mystagogy—the art and discipline of instruction and interpretation of the mystery of the sacraments the newly baptized have experienced and of the new life of faith and service into which they have been initiated. In a more general sense, mystagogy includes continuing exploration and interpretation of the meaning and significance of our being joined to Christ and his mission. *Mystagogical* is the adjective form of the word and refers to the character or focus of instruction after baptism. *Catechesis* is the word for the process of instruction and formation for those the church prepares for baptism.

Oratory—a place in one's home or workplace set aside for prayer, particularly for praying the daily office of the church. In Latin, *ora* is the word for prayer.

Ordo—a shorthand word for the historic and essential structures and services of Christian worship. Reference to *ordo* is a way of saying, "Out of all the diversity of practices, services, and ways Christians have and do worship, these are the core and center."

Paschal mystery (Easter mystery)—the risen Christ present and active in the liturgy. This is the heart of the Christian gospel in liturgical experience. By retelling and representing the life, ministry, suffering, death, resurrection, and ascension of Jesus Christ, we share in Christ's redemptive act through the sacraments and in life experience. *Paschal* derives from the Aramaic *pasch* (Greek *pascha*) and refers to the Jewish Passover or the Christian Easter.

Paschal narrative—the story of Christ's passion; his last days of supper, arrest, trial, suffering, death, burial, resurrection, and ascension.

Perichoresis (from the Greek "to move around")—the Trinity's dance of grace and love in which we are invited to participate in liturgy and life.

Presider or president—in this book *presider* or *president* refers to the ordained person who serves as the focal leader in worship, with responsibility for conducting the congregation's celebration of the sacraments, especially Holy Communion.

Presbyter—a person ordained to Word and Sacrament, often called a priest, pastor, elder, minister, etc. Deacons are also ordained ministers but to a different work, specifically Word and Service and assisting the presbyter in leading worship.

Psalmody—the art or practice of singing the Psalms in worship or of setting the Psalms to music.

Responsory/responsories—usually short chants consisting of verses or lines (usually from scripture) sung or said in call-and-response fashion, such as: "The Lord be with you. *And also with you*" or "O God, make speed to save us. *O Lord, make haste to help us.*" In the Lord's Day worship; the daily offices for morning, noon, evening, and night prayer; and other services, there are a number of classic ordinary and seasonal responsories.

Rubrics—ritual or ceremonial directions, usually printed in liturgical books at the beginning of any service, or in the course of the text. The term comes from the Latin *ruber* for "red"—the traditional color of the print used to distinguish it from the text of the ritual.

Triduum—the most holy three days of the Christian calendar commencing at sunset on Holy Thursday (Thursday of Holy Week) and continuing through sunset on Easter Day. During the Triduum the church commemorates Jesus' Last Supper; his arrest, trial, condemnation, crucifixion, death, and burial; and his resurrection.

S E L E C T E D   B I B L I O G R A P H Y

for Further Reading
and Exploration

Benson, Robert. *Daily Prayer: A Simple Plan for Learning to Say the Daily Prayer of the Church*. Raleigh, NC: Carolina Broadcasting and Publishing, Inc., 2006. This resource is a kit (book, DVD, bookmark, and CD) to help beginners grasp daily prayer as a distinctive approach to prayer with the church. Contains aids for praying the daily office.

Felton, Gayle C. *This Holy Mystery: A United Methodist Understanding of Holy Communion*. Nashville: Discipleship Resources, 2005. This is the official teaching statement of The United Methodist Church that Dr. Felton has set within a seven-session study guide.

Hickman, Hoyt L., Don E. Saliers, Lawrence H. Stookey, and James F. White. *The New Handbook of the Christian Year*. Nashville: Abingdon Press, 1992. This comprehensive ecumenical book is primarily for worship planners and leaders, but anyone who wants to know more about the seasons and services of the Christian year will find substantive introductions and commentary.

Martínez, Joel N., and Raquel M. Martínez, authors and compilers. *Fiesta Cristiana: Recursos para la adoración/Resources for Worship.* Nashville: Abingdon Press, 2003. This bilingual resource offers Spanish readers access not only to worship resources for the Christian year but also gives readers significant and accessible commentary and introductions in both languages.

Saliers, Don E. *Worship and Spirituality.* Akron, OH: OSL Publications, 1996. A fresh and lyrical look at life around font, book, and table as central to our human journey.

Stamm, Mark W. *Sacraments and Discipleship: Understanding Baptism and the Lord's Supper in a United Methodist Context.* Nashville: Discipleship Resources, 2001. While specifically oriented to United Methodist understandings of the sacraments, this is a valuable perspective for an ecumenical audience.

Tanner, Carolyn. *This Holy Mystery: A Study Guide for Children and Youth.* Akron, OH: OSL Publications, 2006. Tanner includes the text of *This Holy Mystery*, along with lesson plans and teaching aids for sessions with children and youth.

Vann, Jane Rogers. *Gathered Before God: Worship-Centered Church Renewal.* Louisville, KY: Westminster John Knox Press, 2004. Studying ten churches, Vann proposes that robust church life today happens when churches continuously reflect on the centrality of their encounter with God in worship and shows how such a focus enables growing discernment of God's activity in all of life.

White, Susan J. *The Spirit of Worship: The Liturgical Tradition.* London: Darton, Longman & Todd, 1999. White explores the liturgical tradition in its diversity and its dynamics that shape our lives and prayer. Contains a rich sampling of the voices from the world of liturgical prayer.

White, James F. *Introduction to Christian Worship*, 3rd ed. Nashville: Abingdon Press, 2000. This has become a classic and comprehensive text on worship and is widely used in seminaries.

Willimon, William H. *Remember Who You Are: Baptism, a Model for Christian Life*. Nashville: The Upper Room, 1980. Provocative and challenging in rediscovering the baptismal covenant and its significance for daily living. Includes an educational guide for groups.

———. *Word, Water, Wine and Bread: How Worship Has Changed over the Years*. Valley Forge, PA: Judson Press, 1980. This is a readable story of the history of Christian worship from its Jewish roots to the reforms following Vatican II.

The worship books of your denomination likely contain important commentary and introductions to your church's liturgical and ritual resources. Episcopal: Book of Common Prayer; Evangelical Lutheran Church in America: *Evangelical Lutheran Worship*; The Presbyterian Church (USA) and Cumberland Presbyterian Church: *Book of Common Worship*; United Church of Christ: *Book of Worship: United Church of Christ*; United Methodist: *The United Methodist Book of Worship*.

In addition to these resources, Upper Room Books offers a number of books and other resources keyed to the Christian year and liturgical practice, including books by Wendy M. Wright, Blair Meeks, and the three volumes in the Guide to Prayer series by Rueben P. Job and Norman Shawchuck, as well as *Upper Room Worshipbook: Music and Liturgies for Spiritual Formation*. For more information, see www.upperroom.org/bookstore or call 1-800-972-0433.

The World Wide Web has many sites devoted to worship and liturgy. The following list is not an endorsement of selected sites but an invitation to explore what they offer:

Calvin Institute of Christian Worship:
   http://www.calvin.edu/worship/
Lift Up Your Hearts: http://www.worship.ca/
United Methodist Worship: http://www.gbod.org/worship/
The Text This Week: http://textweek.com/
ELCA Worship: http://www.elca.org/worship/about_worship/

ABOUT THE AUTHOR

D aniel T. Benedict Jr. is a consultant, author, and retired clergy member of the California-Pacific Annual Conference of The United Methodist Church. From 1993 to 2005 he served as director of worship resourcing for the General Board of Discipleship (GBOD) of The United Methodist Church. Before coming to the GBOD, he served for thirty years as a pastor of congregations in New York and California. Dan is the author of *Come to the Waters: Baptism and Our Ministry of Welcoming Seekers and Making Disciples* and coauthor with Craig Kennet Miller of *Contemporary Worship for the 21st Century: Worship or Evangelism?* He has also published articles in *Worship Arts, Doxology, Sacramental Life, Discipleship Quarterly, Catechumenate,* and *Liturgy*.

Dan's educational background includes a BA in history and religion from Syracuse University, an MDiv from American Baptist Seminary of the West, and additional studies at

Claremont School of Theology. Dan is a longtime member of the Order of Saint Luke, The Fellowship of United Methodists in Worship and the Arts, the North American Association for the Catechumenate, the Consultation on Common Texts, and The North American Academy of Liturgy.

Dan and his wife, Mary O, have two grown children and five grandchildren. Dan's hobbies include walking the beaches, watching movies, woodworking, cooking, and surfing the Internet.